JAMESTOWN DOCUMENTS

A VOYAGE TO VIRGINIA IN 1609

Two Narratives

Strachey's "True Reportory"

and

Jourdain's *Discovery of the Bermudas*

*Published with the assistance of
the Jamestown Foundation*

A
VOYAGE TO VIRGINIA
IN 1609

Two Narratives

Strachey's "True Reportory"
and
Jourdain's *Discovery of the Bermudas*

EDITED BY
LOUIS B. WRIGHT

PUBLISHED FOR
*The Association for the Preservation
of Virginia Antiquities*

THE UNIVERSITY PRESS OF VIRGINIA
Charlottesville

Jan., 1965

Library of Congress Catalog Card Number: 64-19202

*Printed in the United States of America by
The Dietz Press, Inc.*

PREFACE

THE two works reprinted here, inaugurating a projected series of contemporary narratives relating to the settlement of Virginia, have been much discussed as sources of Shakespeare's *The Tempest*. Both William Strachey and Silvester Jourdain were passengers on the ill-fated "Sea Venture," which wrecked in 1609 within sight of one of the Bermuda Islands when this vessel, with eight others in the expedition led by Sir Thomas Gates, was on its way to Jamestown. Aside from their Virginian and Shakespearean interest, the narratives that Strachey and Jourdain wrote are both intrinsically fascinating documents and have a significant place in the voyage literature of their day.

To make for easier reading, they are reprinted here for the first time with the spelling, punctuation, and capitalization modernized. Obvious printing errors have been silently corrected but all obsolete words have been retained. The text, except for these changes, is faithful to the first printed editions.

The editor is indebted to Miss Virginia LaMar, co-editor of the Folger Library General Reader's Shakespeare, for invaluable assistance with both text and notes and to Mrs. John D. Hendrickson for help in the preparation of the manuscript.

L. B. W.

November 15, 1963

CONTENTS

Preface v

Introduction ix

William Strachey, "A True Reportory of the
    Wreck and Redemption of Sir Thomas
    Gates, Knight" 1

Silvester Jourdain, *A Discovery of the Ber-
    mudas, Otherwise Called the Isle of Devils* 103

INTRODUCTION

HEN William Shakespeare sat down to write *The Tempest* he had fresh in his memory a vivid description of a hurricane and shipwreck from the pen of a passenger on the ill-fated ship, the "Sea Venture,"[1] that foundered, en route to Virginia, in a tropical storm off the Bermuda Islands on July 28, 1609. The author was William Strachey, a gentleman-adventurer, one of a company of more than 600 colonists bound for Jamestown, who set out from Plymouth, England, on June 2, 1609, in seven ships and two pinnaces. The flagship of the fleet was the "Sea Venture," commanded by Captain Christopher Newport, who had led the first expedition to Jamestown two years before. On board the "Sea Venture" were Sir Thomas Gates, who had been appointed governor of the colony of Virginia pending the arrival of Lord De La Warr, and Sir

[1] The name of the ship is given in contemporary documents as both the "Sea Venture" and the "Sea Adventure."

George Somers, who held the title of admiral of the
flotilla. Using timbers and materials from their wrecked
ship, supplemented by cedarwood from Bermuda, the
castaways managed to build two seaworthy vessels in
which they eventually reached Virginia. Strachey wrote
an account of their experiences, in the form of a long
letter addressed to an unidentified noble lady, and sent
it back from Virginia. It was this letter that Shakespeare had obviously read before writing *The Tempest*.
The letter was not published in Shakespeare's lifetime
but first appeared in print in Samuel Purchas' *Pilgrims*
(1625) with the title, "A true reportory of the wracke,
and redemption of Sir Thomas Gates Knight; upon,
and from the Ilands of the Bermudas: his comming to
Virginia, and the estate of that Colonie then, and after,
under the government of the Lord La Warre, July 15.
1610. written by William Strachey, Esquire."[2]

The identity of the noble lady is a matter of con-
jecture. Dr. S. G. Culliford in an unpublished dissertation, "William Strachey, 1572-1621," suggests that
the recipient of the letter was Sara, wife of Sir Thomas
Smith, treasurer of the Virginia Company of London.
This is plausible, for Strachey was himself obviously in
the good graces of officials of the company and a little
later was made secretary of the colony at Jamestown.

[2]The letter or "True Reportory" is printed in the modern edition of
Samuel Purchas, *Hakluytus Posthumus, or Purchas His Pilgrims* (Glas-
gow, 1906), XIX, 5-72.

It would be reasonable for him to address an account of the shipwreck and of the subsequent adventures of the castaways on the island to the wife of his prospective patron.

Shakespeare also had connections with members of the Virginia Company. His own patron, the Earl of Southampton, was one of the promoters of the enterprise, as were two other noblemen who befriended him, William Herbert, Earl of Pembroke, and Philip Herbert, Earl of Montgomery. Strachey himself had moved in the literary circle that included Shakespeare. He was a friend of Ben Jonson and was a shareholder in an acting company known as the Children of the Queen's Revels, which had rented the Blackfriars playhouse from Shakespeare's colleague Richard Burbage. In a small group of this sort Strachey's erstwhile friends would have heard something of his adventures. If the letter addressed to the noble lady did not circulate in manuscript in this group, they would at least have known about the substance of it. The expedition led by Gates was the largest that had yet gone out to Virginia, and news of the disaster that befell it created great excitement throughout London, particularly among the shareholders in Shakespeare's circle who stood to lose large sums on their investment.

Strachey, who wrote so dramatically of the wreck of the "Sea Venture," was a native of Saffron Walden in

Essex, where his family belonged to the minor gentry.[3]
He was born in 1572; in 1588, the year of the Armada,
he entered Emmanuel College, Cambridge. Records do
not show whether he graduated. In 1595 he married
Frances Forster of Crowhurst in Surrey. By 1605 he
was living in London and was a member of Gray's Inn,
where he had an opportunity of meeting many rising
young lawyers and men of letters. He himself dabbled
in literature, and we have a few evidences of his interest
in poetry at this time. Among his verses is a sonnet
prefatory to Ben Jonson's tragedy *Sejanus*. Thomas
Campion, a fellow member of Gray's Inn, addressed to
him an epigram, *Ad Guglielmum Stracheum*.

In 1606 Strachey obtained a post as secretary to
Thomas Glover, then about to sail for Constantinople
as ambassador to the Sublime Porte. The ambassador
whom Glover succeeded was Henry Lello, a scholarly
man of letters, who claimed that Glover had displaced
him by underhanded means and declined to leave Constantinople. Strachey on the voyage outbound quickly
discovered that Glover was a disagreeable person and
on arrival in Constantinople he made friends with
Lello. Finding such disloyal conduct impossible to for-

[3]For a brief account of Strachey's career, see the introduction to *The
Historie of Travell into Virginia Britania (1612),* edited by Louis B.
Wright and Virginia Freund (London: Hakluyt Society, 1953), pp.
xvii ff. The most detailed study of Strachey is that by Culliford cited
earlier, a doctoral dissertation submitted to the University of London
in 1950.

give, Glover dismissed Strachey, who made his way to Venice, where he sought in vain to find employment with the English ambassador, Sir Henry Wotton.

Strachey got back to London about a year before Sir Thomas Gates's expedition set out for Virginia. Since no gainful employment offered itself, he volunteered to go and took passage on the "Sea Venture." There is no evidence that he had been promised any office in the colony, but he evidently enjoyed the companionship and favor of the leaders. Later at Jamestown, Strachey was given the post of Matthew Scrivener, the secretary of the colony, who had drowned in January, 1609.

The voyage of the fleet of nine vessels was uneventful until they were within a week's sailing time of the Virginia coast. Then, on the night of July 23, heavy clouds foretold a storm of unusual intensity. The morning brought a hurricane from the northeast, "which," says Strachey, "swelling and roaring as it were by fits, some hours with more violence than others, at length did beat all light from Heaven; which, like an hell of darkness, turned black upon us." The fleet was scattered. After battling winds and waves for four days and nights, the "Sea Venture" was at last driven upon the shore of an island, which to the horror of superstitious sailors turned out to be one of the Bermudas, already ill-famed as the "Isle of Devils." By sheer luck the ship was wedged between two rocks so that it did not capsize or sink. Manning their boats, the crew and

passengers got ashore safely. Furthermore they sal-
vaged such stores as had not been spoiled by sea water,
and they brought ashore all their tools and implements.
These were to prove their salvation, for during their
stay of eleven months in the islands they were able to
fashion timbers and planks with which they built the
two vessels, the "Deliverance" and the "Patience," that
took them to Virginia.

Strachey made his description of the hurricane, the
wreck, and life on the islands factually accurate without
diminishing its vividness. Nor did he gloss over unpleasant details. His narration of the shortcomings of
some of the group and the mutinies that nearly ruined
their prospects of escaping from the Bermudas were
not matters that the Virginia Company of London
would want to publish abroad. These comments are
sufficient to explain why Strachey's report had to wait
until 1625 to see print. That does not mean, however,
that the officials of the company did not read carefully
all that he had written and give heed to the implications
between the lines. Strachey makes clear that the quality
of some of the emigrants helped to explain the difficulties experienced in trying to establish a successful base
at Jamestown. The mutinies described by Strachey also
provided suggestions to Shakespeare for the mutinous
sailors in *The Tempest*.

When the castaways in their two vessels reached
Jamestown, they were pleased to learn that all the other

vessels in the fleet except one pinnace had avoided com-
plete disaster and had at last limped into port. But they
were appalled at the state of the colony. Most of the
emigrants had died of disease and near-starvation during the preceding winter when the crew and passengers
of the "Sea Venture" were living comfortably and well
in the sunny Bermudas. Besieged by Indians, who kept
the settlers penned within their stockade, the colonists
could neither hunt nor fish successfully. They could not
even venture out to gather wood without the risk of
death from an Indian's arrow or tomahawk. On his
arrival Gates had accepted the resignation of George
Percy, brother of the Earl of Northumberland, who
had been serving as a less than successful governor.
Gates did his best to salvage the depressed colony, but
the shortage of food and the scarcity of competent men
at last forced him to conclude that they must abandon
Jamestown. In two pinnaces and the two vessels built
in Bermuda they would try to reach Newfoundland,
where they could hope to obtain passage home in the
fishing fleet. Accordingly they embarked on June 7,
1610, but before they arrived at the open sea they met
a longboat from the fleet of Lord De La Warr, who
was coming with reinforcements and supplies. At this
news Gates put about and returned to Jamestown. The
colony was saved.

Lord De La Warr brought his fleet to anchor at
Jamestown and immediately set to work to reorganize

the colony. On June 12 he made a public announcement of his council and officers. These included William Strachey as secretary and recorder. Lord De La Warr made plain his condemnation of indolence and incompetence, for, Strachey reported, he "delivered some few words unto the company, laying many blames upon them for many vanities and their idleness, earnestly wishing that he might no more find it so lest he should be compelled to draw the sword of justice to cut off such delinquents."

The colony at Jamestown was not yet a success, but it would never again fall to the low state that it reached prior to Lord De La Warr's arrival. From this time onward the Virginia enterprise would slowly gain momentum. Strachey's letter was taken to London by Sir Thomas Gates, who sailed about the middle of July, 1610. Perhaps the unvarnished truths that Strachey reported helped to open the eyes of officials at home to the necessity of better planning and a more discriminating selection of prospective settlers.

Strachey himself returned to England in the early autumn of 1611 and was doubtless called into consultation by officials of the Virginia Company of London. His first literary task after his return was to edit a body of laws proclaimed at Jamestown by Gates, Lord De La Warr, and Sir Thomas Dale, who succeeded De La Warr. The compilation bearing the title *For the Colony in Virginia Britannia: Laws Divine, Moral, and Martial* was published in 1612. It was dedicated to the officers and members of the Virginia Company and dated from the editor's lodgings in the Blackfriars. Strachey expressed his willingness to serve the company either at home or by returning to Jamestown, but there is no evidence that he ever went back to Virginia. Instead he immediately set about compiling *The History of Travel into Virginia Britannia,* which he planned to make into a great anthology of narratives of English exploration along the Atlantic littoral, but he changed his mind at some point, and near the end of 1612 he brought the manuscript to an abrupt conclusion. He borrowed from various earlier travel narratives and added some observations of his own but missed the opportunity of giving a full account of what he himself saw and experienced. In this narrative Strachey did not repeat the story he had related in the "True Reportory." The manuscript, which exists in three states, was never published until the Hakluyt Society version edited by R. H. Major appeared in 1849. A new edition was published by the Hakluyt Society in 1953.

Strachey lived out his life in London but never succeeded in obtaining any substantial advancement or recognition. He married a second wife, but all we know about her is her first name, Dorothy. On June 21, 1621, the parish register of St. Giles, Camberwell, records the burial of William Strachey. In his later years Strachey had given himself to moralizing piety, and the Bodleian Library possesses a manuscript listed as "Mr. Strachey's Hark" which begins:

> Hark! 'Twas the trump of death that blew.
> My hour is come. False world adieu.
> Thy pleasures have betrayed me so
> That I to death untimely go.[4]

Strachey died unaware that his letter to a noble lady would live in aftertime because it inspired one of Shakespeare's most fascinating plays.

Another account of the wreck of the "Sea Venture" that deserves preservation is Silvester Jourdain's *A Discovery of the Bermudas, Otherwise Called the Isle of Devils,* printed in London by John Windet for the bookseller Roger Barnes in 1610.[5] It confirms Strachey's account of the trials of the Virginia-bound voyagers and, like Strachey's work, was read by Shakespeare before he wrote *The Tempest.* Jourdain was also a passenger in the "Sea Venture" and his narrative has a few colorful details not mentioned by Strachey. For example, he records that some of the ship's company, after four days of pumping and bailing, gave up hope of saving themselves from sinking and, "having some

---

[4]The Bodleian MS is Ashmole MS 781.f.135. See Charles R. Sanders, "William Strachey, the Virginia Company, and Shakespeare," *Virginia Magazine of History and Biography,* LVII (1949), 115-132.

[5]Jourdain's work, with an introduction by Joseph Quincy Adams, was reproduced by Scholars' Facsimiles and Reprints (New York, 1940).

good and comfortable waters in the ship, fetched them and drunk one to the other, taking their last leave one of the other until their more joyful and happy meeting in a more blessed world." The solace of these "comfortable waters" may have suggested the consolation that Trinculo and his companions found in their cache of liquor in *The Tempest*.

Jourdain's work was the first published account of the disaster and served to whet the public interest in this episode. Since he did not elaborate upon unfavorable details of the stay in Bermuda or the plight of the Jamestown colony, the Virginia Company allowed his narrative to be printed. It ends with the departure of Sir George Somers in his Bermuda-built pinnace on a return journey to the islands to procure hogs and other food for the settlers. From this journey Somers never came back.

Jourdain's account appeared in a second edition without his name entitled *A Plain Description of the Bermudas Now Called the Summer Islands* (1613). This edition had a pious preface by the preacher William Crashaw, one of the great propagandists for the Virginia Company, and it added a further description of the resources of Bermuda "lately sent from thence." It also included a "Copy of Articles" adopted by recent settlers on Bermuda to ensure good behavior.

Jourdain was a native of Lyme Regis in Dorsetshire. His brother Ignatius was a well-to-do merchant of

Exeter and a member of Parliament. Silvester Jourdain himself may have been a merchant of sorts, for the Port Book of Poole lists a shipper of that name in 1603. Jourdain seems to have been a partisan of Sir George Somers, himself a native and resident of Lyme Regis. Of Jourdain's later career little is known. There is a record of the death of a man of his name in the parish of St. Sepulchre, near Newgate, London, in 1650. The present printing of his *Discovery* is based on a copy of the first edition in the Folger Shakespeare Library.

A True Reportory of the Wreck and Redemption of Sir Thomas Gates, Knight, upon and from the Islands of the Bermudas: His Coming to Virginia and the Estate of that Colony Then and After, under the Government of the Lord La Warr, July 15, 1610, written by William Strachey, Esquire

*A most dreadful tempest (the manifold deaths whereof
are here to the life described), their wreck on Bermuda,
and the description of those islands*

XCELLENT LADY, Know that upon
Friday late in the evening we brake
ground out of the sound of Plymouth,
our whole fleet then consisting of seven
good ships and two pinnaces, all which
from the said second of June unto the twenty-third of
July kept in friendly consort together, not a whole
watch at any time losing the sight each of other. Our
course, when we came about the height of between 26
and 27 degrees, we declined to the northward and, according to our governor's instructions, altered the trade
and ordinary way used heretofore by Dominica and
Nevis in the West Indies and found the wind to this
course indeed as friendly as in the judgment of all seamen it is upon a more direct line and by Sir George
Somers our admiral had been likewise in former time
sailed, being a gentleman of approved assuredness and
ready knowledge in seafaring actions, having often

carried command and chief charge in many ships royal
of Her Majesty's and in sundry voyages made many
defeats and attempts in the time of the Spaniard's quar-
reling with us upon the islands and Indies, etc.

We had followed this course so long as now we were
within seven or eight days at the most, by Captain Newport's reckoning, of making Cape Henry upon the coast
of Virginia, when on St. James his day, July 24, being
Monday (preparing for no less all the black night before),[1] the clouds gathering thick upon us and the winds
singing and whistling most unusually (which made us
to cast off our pinnace, towing the same until then
astern), a dreadful storm and hideous began to blow
from out the northeast, which, swelling and roaring as
it were by fits, some hours with more violence than
others, at length did beat all light from Heaven; which,
like an hell of darkness, turned black upon us, so much
the more fuller of horror as in such cases horror and
fear use to overrun the troubled and overmastered
senses of all, which taken up with amazement, the ears
lay so sensible to the terrible cries and murmurs of the
winds and distraction of our company as who was most
armed and best prepared was not a little shaken.

For surely, noble Lady, as death comes not so sudden

[1]Marginal comment: "A terrible storm expressed in a pathetical and
rhetorical description." Most of the marginal notes accompanying
Purchas' printing of Strachey's narrative merely summarize the text and
consequently have been omitted.

nor apparent, so he comes not so elvish[2] and painful (to men, especially, even then in health and perfect habitudes of body) as at sea; who comes at no time so welcome but our frailty (so weak is the hold of hope in miserable demonstrations of danger) it makes guilty of many contrary changes and conflicts. For, indeed, death is accompanied at no time nor place with circumstances every way so uncapable of particularities of goodness and inward comforts as at sea. For it is most true, there ariseth commonly no such unmerciful tempest, compound of so many contrary and divers nations [? motions], but that it worketh upon the whole frame of the body and most loathsomely affecteth all the powers thereof. And the manner of the sickness it lays upon the body, being so unsufferable, gives not the mind any free and quiet time to use her judgment and empire; which made the poet say:

> *Hostium uxores, puerique caecos*
> *Sentiant motus orientis Haedi, et*
> *Aequoris nigri fremitum, et trementes*
> *Verbere ripas.*[3]

[2]Spitefully.

[3]"May the wives and children of our foes be the ones to feel the blind onset of rising Auster and the roaring of the darkling sea, and the shores quivering with the shock!" (Horace *Odes* iii.27.21-24). Where *Haedi* appears in Strachey's quotation, the original reads *Austri* (the south wind). The translation is that of C. E. Bennett for the Loeb edition (New York: Harvard University Press, 1939).

For four-and-twenty hours the storm in a restless tumult had blown so exceedingly as we could not apprehend in our imaginations any possibility of greater violence; yet did we still find it not only more terrible but more constant, fury added to fury, and one storm urging a second more outrageous than the former, whether it so wrought upon our fears or indeed met with new forces. Sometimes strikes [? shrieks] in our ship amongst women and passengers not used to such hurly and discomforts made us look one upon the other with troubled hearts and panting bosoms, our clamors drowned in the winds and the winds in thunder. Prayers might well be in the heart and lips but drowned in the outcries of the officers:[4] nothing heard that could give comfort, nothing seen that might encourage hope. It is impossible for me, had I the voice of Stentor and expression of as many tongues as his throat of voices, to express the outcries and miseries, not languishing but wasting his spirits, and art constant to his own principles but not prevailing.

Our sails wound up lay without their use, and if at any time we bore but a hullock,[5] or half forecourse, to guide her before the sea, six and sometimes eight men were not enough to hold the whipstaff[6] in the steerage

---

[4]Compare *The Tempest* (I,i): "(*Cry Within*) A plague upon this howling! They are louder than the weather or our office."

[5]Scrap of sail.

[6]The lever by which the ship was steered; the lower end connected with the tiller and controlled the rudder of the ship.

and the tiller below in the gunner room: by which may
be imagined the strength of the storm, in which the sea
swelled above the clouds and gave battle unto Heaven.[7]
It could not be said to rain: the waters like whole rivers
did flood in the air. And this I did still observe: that
whereas upon the land when a storm hath poured itself
forth once in drifts of rain, the wind, as beaten down
and vanquished therewith, not long after endureth; here
the glut of water (as if throttling the wind erewhile)
was no sooner a little emptied and qualified but instantly
the winds (as having gotten their mouths now free and
at liberty) spake more loud and grew more tumultuous
and malignant.[8] What shall I say? Winds and seas
were as mad as fury and rage could make them. For
my own part, I had been in some storms before, as well
upon the coast of Barbary and Algiers, in the Levant,
and once, more distressful, in the Adriatic gulf in a
bottom of Candy,[9] so as I may well say: *Ego quid sit
ater Hadriae novi sinus, et quid albus peccet Iapyx.*[10]
Yet all that I had ever suffered gathered together might

[7]Marginal comment: "Swelling sea set forth in a swelling style."

[8]See *The Tempest* (I,i): "Though every drop of water gape at
widest to *glut* him." The word "glut" is not used elsewhere by
Shakespeare.

[9]Bottom of Candy: Cretan vessel.

[10]"Full well I know what Hadria's [the Adriatic's] black gulf can
be and what the sins of clear Iapyx [the northwest wind]" (Horace
Odes iii.27.18-19). This is C. E. Bennett's translation for the Loeb
edition cited above.

not hold comparison with this: there was not a moment in which the sudden splitting or instant oversetting of the ship was not expected.

Howbeit this was not all. It pleased God to bring a greater affliction yet upon us; for in the beginning of the storm we had received likewise a mighty leak. And the ship, in every joint almost having spewed out her oakum before we were aware (a casualty more desperate than any other that a voyage by sea draweth with it), was grown five foot suddenly deep with water above her ballast, and we almost drowned within whilst we sat looking when to perish from above. This, imparting no less terror than danger, ran through the whole ship with much fright and amazement, startled and turned the blood and took down the braves[11] of the most hardy mariner of them all, insomuch as he that before happily felt not the sorrow of others now began to sorrow for himself, when he saw such a pond of water so suddenly broken in and which he knew could not (without present avoiding[12]) but instantly sink him. So as joining (only for his own sake, not yet worth the saving) in the public safety there might be seen master, master's mate, boatswain, quartermaster, coopers, carpenters, and who not, with candles in their hands, creeping along the ribs viewing the sides, searching every corner, and listening in every place if they could hear

[11]Bravados.
[12]Immediate bailing out.

the water run. Many a weeping leak was this way found and hastily stopped, and at length one in the gunner room made up with I know not how many pieces of beef. But all was to no purpose; the leak (if it were but one) which drunk in our greatest seas and took in our destruction fastest could not then be found, nor ever was, by any labor, counsel, or search. The waters still increasing and the pumps going, which at length choked with bringing up whole and continual biscuit (and indeed all we had, ten thousandweight), it was conceived as most likely that the leak might be sprung in the bread room; whereupon the carpenter went down and ripped up all the room but could not find it so.

I am not able to give unto Your Ladyship every man's thought in this perplexity to which we were now brought; but to me this leakage appeared as a wound given to men that were before dead. The Lord knoweth, I had as little hope as desire of life in the storm, and in this: it went beyond my will because beyond my reason why we should labor to preserve life. Yet we did, either because so dear are a few lingering hours of life in all mankind, or that our Christian knowledges taught us how much we owed to the rites of nature, as bound not to be false to ourselves or to neglect the means of our own preservation, the most despairful things amongst men being matters of no wonder nor moment with Him Who is the rich fountain and admirable essence of all mercy.

Our governor, upon the Tuesday morning (at what time, by such who had been below in the hold, the leak was first discovered) had caused the whole company, about 140, besides women, to be equally divided into three parts and, opening the ship in three places (under the forecastle, in the waist, and hard by the bittacle[13]), appointed each man where to attend; and thereunto every man came duly upon his watch, took the bucket or pump for one hour, and rested another. Then men might be seen to labor, I may well say, for life; and the better sort, even our governor and admiral themselves, not refusing their turn and to spell each the other, to give example to other. The common sort, stripped naked as men in galleys, the easier both to hold out and to shrink from under the salt water which continually leapt in among them, kept their eyes waking and their thoughts and hands working with tired bodies and wasted spirits three days and four nights, destitute of outward comfort and desperate of any deliverance, testifying how mutually willing they were yet by labor to keep each other from drowning, albeit each one drowned whilst he labored.

Once so huge a sea brake upon the poop and quarter upon us as it covered our ship from stern to stem like a garment or a vast cloud; it filled her brim full for a while within, from the hatches up to the spardeck. The source or confluence of water was so violent as it rushed

[13]Compass box. The modern word "binnacle" is a corruption.

and carried the helm-man from the helm and wrested
the whipstaff out of his hand, which so flew from side
to side that when he would have seized the same again
it so tossed him from starboard to larboard as it was
God's mercy it had not split him. It so beat him from
his hold and so bruised him as a fresh man hazarding
in by chance fell fair with it and, by main strength bearing somewhat up, made good[14] his place and with much
clamor encouraged and called upon others, who gave
her now up, rent in pieces and absolutely lost. Our
governor was at this time below at the capstan, both by
his speech and authority heartening every man unto his
labor. It struck him from the place where he sat and
groveled him and all us about him on our faces, beating
together with our breaths all thoughts from our bosoms
else than that we were now sinking. For my part, I
thought her already in the bottom of the sea; and I
have heard him say, wading out of the flood thereof,
all his ambition was but to climb up above-hatches to
die in *aperto coelo* and in the company of his old
friends. It so stunned the ship in her full pace that she
stirred no more than if she had been caught in a net,
or than as if the fabulous remora[15] had stuck to her
forecastle. Yet, without bearing one inch of sail, even
then she was making her way nine or ten leagues in a

[14]Made good: supplied.

[15]A marginal note explains, "Remora is fabled to be a small fish able
to withstand a ship in her course."

watch. One thing it is not without his wonder (whether it were the fear of death in so great a storm, or that it pleased God to be gracious unto us), there was not a passenger, gentleman or other, after he began to stir and labor, but was able to relieve his fellow and make good his course. And it is most true, such as in all their lifetimes had never done hour's work before (their minds now helping their bodies) were able twice forty-eight hours together to toil with the best.

During all this time the heavens looked so black upon us that it was not possible the elevation of the Pole might be observed; nor a star by night nor sunbeam by day was to be seen. Only upon the Thursday night Sir George Somers, being upon the watch, had an apparition of a little, round light, like a faint star, trembling and streaming along with a sparkling blaze, half the height upon the main mast and shooting sometimes from shroud to shroud, 'tempting to settle, as it were, upon any of the four shrouds. And for three or four hours together, or rather more, half the night, it kept with us, running sometimes along the main yard to the very end and then returning;[16] at which Sir George Somers called divers about him and showed them the

[16]Compare Ariel's description of his activities: "Now on the beak, / Now in the waist, the deck, in every cabin, / I flamed amazement. Sometimes I'ld divide / And burn in many places; on the topmast, / The yards, and bowsprit would I flame distinctly, / Then meet and join" (*Tempest,* I,ii).

same, who observed it with much wonder and carefulness.[17]   But upon a sudden, toward the morning watch, they lost the sight of it and knew not what way it made.

The superstitious seamen make many constructions of this sea fire, which nevertheless is usual in storms, the same (it may be) which the Grecians were wont in the Mediterranean to call Castor and Pollux, of which if one only appeared without the other they took it for an evil sign of great tempest.   The Italians and such who lie open to the Adriatic and Tyrrhenian Sea call it (a sacred body) *corpo sancto;* the Spaniards call it St. Elmo and have an authentic and miraculous legend for it.   Be it what it will, we laid other foundations of safety or ruin than in the rising or falling of it.   Could it have served us now miraculously to have taken our height by, it might have strucken amazement and a reverence in our devotions according to the due of a miracle.   But it did not light us any whit the more to our known way, who ran now (as do hoodwinked[18] men) at all adventures, sometimes north and northeast, then north and by west, and in an instant again varying two or three points, and sometimes half the compass. East and by south we steered away as much as we could to bear upright, which was no small carefulness nor pain to do, albeit we much unrigged our ship, threw overboard much luggage, many a trunk and chest (in

[17]Anxiety.
[18]Blindfolded.

which I suffered no mean loss), and staved[19] many a
butt of beer, hogsheads of oil, cider, wine, and vinegar,
and heaved away all our ordnance on the starboard
side, and had now purposed to have cut down the main
mast the more to lighten her, for we were much spent
and our men so weary as their strengths together failed
them with their hearts, having travailed now from
Tuesday till Friday morning, day and night, without
either sleep or food; for, the leakage taking up all the
hold, we could neither come by beer nor fresh water;
fire we could keep none in the cook room to dress any
meat; and carefulness, grief, and our turn at the pump
or bucket were sufficient to hold sleep from our eyes.

And surely, madam, it is most true, there was not
any hour (a matter of admiration[20]) all these days in
which we freed not twelve hundred barricos[21] of water,
the least whereof contained six gallons, and some eight;
besides three deep pumps continually going, two be-
neath at the capstan and the other above in the half
deck, and at each pump four thousand strokes at the
least in a watch. So as I may well say, every four hours
we quitted one hundred tons of water. And from Tuesday noon till Friday noon we bailed and pumped two
thousand ton; and yet, do what we could, when our
ship held least in her (after Tuesday night second

[19]Broke open and emptied.
[20]Wonder.
[21]Kegs.

watch), she bore ten foot deep; at which stay our extreme working kept her one eight glasses,[22] forbearance whereof had instantly sunk us. And it being now Friday, the fourth morning, it wanted little but that there had been a general determination to have shut up hatches and, commending our sinful souls to God, committed the ship to the mercy of the gale. Surely, that night we must have done it, and that night had we then perished. But see the goodness and sweet introduction of better hope by our merciful God given unto us: Sir George Somers, when no man dreamed of such happiness, had discovered and cried land.

Indeed the morning, now three quarters spent, had won a little clearness from the days before, and it being better surveyed, the very trees were seen to move with the wind upon the shoreside; whereupon our governor commanded the helm-man to bear up. The boatswain, sounding at the first, found it thirteen fathom, and when we stood [in] a little, in seven fathom; and presently, heaving his lead the third time, had ground at four fathom; and by this we had got her within a mile under the southeast point of the land, where we had somewhat smooth water. But having no hope to save her by coming to an anchor in the same, we were enforced to run her ashore as near the land as we could, which brought us within three quarters of a mile of

[22]That is, continual pumping kept her water level at ten feet for four hours (a revolution of eight glasses by nautical timekeeping).

shore; and by the mercy of God unto us, making out our boats, we had ere night brought all our men, women, and children, about the number of 150, safe into the island.

We found it to be the dangerous and dreaded island, or rather islands, of the Bermuda; whereof let me give Your Ladyship a brief description before I proceed to my narration. And that the rather because they be so terrible to all that ever touched on them, and such tempests, thunders, and other fearful objects are seen and heard about them, that they be called commonly the Devil's Islands and are feared and avoided of all sea travelers alive above any other place in the world. Yet it pleased our merciful God to make even this hideous and hated place both the place of our safety and means of our deliverance.

And hereby, also, I hope to deliver the world from a foul and general error, it being counted of most that they can be no habitation for men but rather given over to devils and wicked spirits; whereas indeed we find them now by experience to be as habitable and commodious as most countries of the same climate and situation, insomuch as, if the entrance into them were as easy as the place itself is contenting, it had long ere this been inhabited as well as other islands. Thus shall we make it appear that Truth is the daughter of Time, and that men ought not to deny everything which is not subject to their own sense.

The Bermudas be broken islands, five hundred of them in manner of an archipelago (at least if you may call them all islands that lie, how little soever, into the sea and by themselves) of small compass, some larger yet than other, as time and the sea hath won from them and eaten his passage through; and all now lying in the figure of a croissant, within the circuit of six or seven leagues at the most, albeit at first it is said of them that they were thirteen or fourteen leagues, and more in longitude, as I have heard. For no greater distance is it from the northwest point to Gates his bay, as by this map[23] Your Ladyship may see; in which Sir George Somers, who coasted in his boat about them all, took great care to express the same exactly and full and made his draft perfect for all good occasions and the benefit of such who either in distress might be brought upon them or make sail this way.

[23]Purchas adds a marginal note: "Sir George Somers' diligent survey; his draft which we have not. M. Norgate hath since published an exact map." "M. Norgate" is Richard Norwood, who made an official survey of the islands in 1618 and wrote a description of the islands. The Stationers' Register contains an entry, dated January 19, 1621/22, for "A Plot or Map of Bermudas or the Summer Islands Made by Richard Norwood." If the map was separately printed, no copies seem to be known, but Captain John Smith used the text and printed a copy of the map in *The General History of Virginia, New England, and the Summer Islands* (1624), and Samuel Purchas also printed the description in *Purchas His Pilgrims* (1624-25), IV, 1796-1800. For further details see the "Bibliography of Norwood's Writings" by William A. Jackson in *The Journal of Richard Norwood, Surveyor of Bermuda* (New York, 1945), pp. lix-lx.

It should seem, by the testimony of Gonzalus Ferdinandus Oviedus[24] in his book entitled *The Summary or Abridgment of His General History of the West Indies,* written to the Emperor Charles the Fifth, that they have been indeed of greater compass (and I easily believe it) than they are now; who thus saith:

In the year 1515, when I came first to inform Your Majesty of the state of the things in India, and was the year following in Flanders in the time of your most fortunate success in these your kingdoms of Aragon and Castile, whereas at that voyage I sailed above the island Bermudas, otherwise called Garza, being the farthest of all the island that are yet found at this day in the world, and arriving there at the depth of eight yards[25] of water and distant from the land as far as the shot of a piece of ordnance, I determined to send some of the ship to land, as well to make search of such things as were there as also to leave in the island certain hogs for increase; but the time not serving my purpose, by reason of contrary wind, I could bring my ships no nearer the island, being twelve leagues

[24]It has been conjectured that Oviedo's given names suggested to Shakespeare the names "Gonzalo" and "Ferdinand" for characters in *The Tempest.*

[25]Purchas has a marginal note: "Or fadams braccia. In his *Gen. Hist., lib.* 2, *cap.* 9, he reciteth the same history more particularly. He saith it hath two names, Garza, of the ship which first discovered it, being so called, and Bermudez, of the captain of that ship, named John Bermudez. Note that he placeth it more to the north than that which is by ours inhabited and says sometime they see it, sometime not, as they pass. The Spaniards (as I have heard) which were wrecked there in Captain Butler's time were of opinion that ours are not the Bermudas. Yea, some of ours affirm they have seen such an island to the north of ours and have offered to discover it. *Sub iudice list est:*

in length and sixteen[26] in breadth and about thirty in circuit, lying in the 33 degrees of the north side.[27]

Thus far he.

True it is, the main island, or greatest of them now, may be some sixteen miles in length east-northeast and west-southwest, the longest part of it standing in 32 degrees and 20 minutes; in which is a great bay on the north side, in the northwest end, and many broken

---

Veritas Temporis filia [Judiciously it is said, 'Truth is the daughter of Time']." *Braccia* is an Italian nautical measure, but it is not clear whether Purchas means to equate yards, fathoms, and *braccia*. The *General History* referred to is a larger work by Oviedo than the one described below and was published in two parts in 1535 and 1557. Captain Butler is the Nathaniel Butler who was governor of Bermuda in 1619-22 and who wrote a "History of the Bermudas" (Sloane MS 750) which remained unpublished until an edition was prepared by J. H. Lefroy for the Hakluyt Society in 1822. General Lefroy mistakenly attributed the anonymous narrative to Captain John Smith.

[26]The breadth of the island is given as six rather than sixteen leagues in the source.

[27]The passage appears in Richard Eden's *The Decades of the New World* (1555), which is substantially a translation of Pietro Martire d'Anghiera's *De orbe novo* (1530) but also contains Gonzalo Fernández de Oviedo y Valdes' *Historia general y natural de las Indias* (Toledo, 1526). S. G. Culliford suggests, however, that Strachey actually used Richard Willes' enlarged edition of Eden entitled *The History of Travel in the East and West Indies* (1577), in view of references in "The History of Travel into Virginia Britannia." For example, a citation of Plato is from an interpolated section in Willes titled "A most ancient testimony of the West Indies by the writing of the divine philosopher Plato" (see the Culliford dissertation already cited, pp. 336-40).

islands in that sound or bay, and a little round island at the southwest end. As occasions were offered, so we gave titles and names to certain places.

These islands are often afflicted and rent with tempests, great strokes of thunder, lightning, and rain in the extremity of violence; which (and it may well be) hath so sundered and torn down the rocks and whirried[28] whole quarters of islands into the main sea (some six, some seven leagues, and is like in time to swallow them all), so as even in that distance from the shore there is no small danger of them, and with them of the storms continually raging from them, which once in the full and change commonly of every moon (winter or summer) keep their unchangeable round and rather thunder than blow from every corner about them, sometimes forty-eight hours together, especially if the circle which the philosophers call halo were (in our being there) seen about the moon at any season, which bow indeed appeared there often and would be of a mighty compass and breadth. I have not observed it anywhere one quarter so great; especially about the twentieth of March I saw the greatest, when followed upon the eve's Eve of the Annunciation of Our Lady the mightiest blast of lightning and most terrible rap of thunder that ever astonied[29] mortal men, I think.

In August, September, and until the end of October

[28]Whirled.
[29]Stunned.

we had very hot and pleasant weather; only (as I say)
thunder, lightning, and many scattering showers of rain
(which would pass swiftly over and yet fall with such
force and darkness for the time as if it would never be
clear again) we wanted not any; and of rain more in
summer than in winter. And in the beginning of December we had great store of hail (the sharp winds
blowing northerly), but it continued not; and to say
truth, it is wintry or summer weather there according
as those north and northwest winds blow. Much taste
of this kind of winter we had; for those cold winds
would suddenly alter the air. But when there was no
breath of wind to bring the moist air out of the seas
from the north and northwest we were rather weary of
the heat than pinched with extremity of cold. Yet the
three winter months, December, January, and February, the winds kept in those cold corners, and indeed
then it was heavy and melancholy being there; nor were
the winds more rough in March than in the foresaid
months; and yet even then would the birds breed. I
think they bred there most months in the year. In September and at Christmas I saw young birds, and in February, at which time the mornings are there (as in May
in England) fresh and sharp.

Well may the Spaniards and these Biscayan pilots,
with all their traders into the Indies, pass by these
islands, as afraid (either bound out or homewards) of
their very meridian, and leave the fishing for the pearl

(which some say, and I believe well, is as good there as in any of their other Indian islands, and whereof we had some trial) to such as will adventure for them. The seas about them are so full of breaches as, with those dangers, they may well be said to be the strongest situate in the world. I have often heard Sir George Somers and Captain Newport say how they have not been by any chance or discovery upon their like. It is impossible without great and perfect knowledge and search first made of them to bring in a bauble[30] boat so much as of ten ton without apparent[31] ruin, albeit within there are many fair harbors for the greatest English ship; yea, the argosies of Venice may ride there with water enough and safe landlocked. There is one only side that admits so much as hope of safety by many a league, on which (as before described) it pleased God to bring us; we had not come one man of us else ashore, as the weather was. They have been ever, therefore, left desolate and not inhabited.

The soil of the whole island is one and the same; the mold dark, red, sandy, dry, and uncapable, I believe, of any of our commodities or fruits.[32] Sir George

[30]Trifling; of small draught.

[31]Certain.

[32]Marginal note: "Experience hath better showed since, as we after see, both for fruits, worms, etc., those that dwell there finding more than these which took there inn or lodging. Yet the dawning and Aurora yield a delightsome light, though not all so certain as the sun; for which cause I have not omitted these first discoveries."

Somers in the beginning of August squared out a garden
by the quarter (the quarter being set down before a
goodly bay upon which our governor did first leap
ashore and therefore called it, as afore said, Gates his
bay, which opened into the east and into which the sea
did ebb and flow according to their tides) and sowed
muskmelons, peas, onions, radish, lettuce, and many
English seeds and kitchen herbs. All which in some ten
days did appear above ground, but whether by the small
birds, of which there be many kinds, or by flies (worms
I never saw any, nor any venomous thing, as toad or
snake or any creeping beast hurtful, only some spiders,
which, as many affirm, are signs of great store of gold;
but they were long and slender-leg spiders, and whether
venomous or no I know not—I believe not, since we
should still find them amongst our linen in our chests
and drinking-cans, but we never received any danger
from them; a kind of melantha or black beetle there
was which bruised gave a savor like many sweet and
strong gums punned[33] together), whether, I say, hin-
dered by these or by the condition or vice of the soil,
they came to no proof nor thrived.

It is like enough that the commodities of the other
western islands would prosper there, as vines, lemons,
oranges, and sugar canes. Our governor made trial of
the latter and buried some two or three in the garden
mold, which were reserved in the wreck amongst many

[33]Pounded.

which we carried to plant here in Virginia, and they began to grow; but the hogs, breaking in, both rooted them up and eat them. There is not through the whole islands either champaign ground, valleys, or fresh rivers. They are full of shaws[34] of goodly cedar, fairer than ours here of Virginia, the berries whereof our men, seething, straining, and letting stand some three or four days, made a kind of pleasant drink.[35] These berries are of the same bigness and color of corinths,[36] full of little stones and very restringent or hard-building.[37] Peter Martin[38] saith that at Alexandria in Egypt there is a kind of cedar which the Jews dwelling there affirm to be the cedars of Libanus, which bear old fruit and new all the year, being a kind of apple which taste like prunes. But then, neither those there in the Bermudas nor ours here in Virginia are of that happy kind.

Likewise there grow great store of palm trees, not the right Indian palms such as in San Juan, Puerto Rico, are called cocos and are there full of small fruits like almonds (of the bigness of the grains in pomegranates), nor of those kind of palms which bear dates, but a kind of simerons or wild palms, in growth, fashion, leaves, and branches resembling those true palms. For

[34]Thickets.

[35]Compare Caliban's mention of "water with berries in it" (*Tempest*, I,ii).

[36]Currants.

[37]Astringent.

[38]Pietro Martire d'Anghiera.

the tree is high and straight, sappy and spongious, un-
firm for any use, no branches but in the uppermost part
thereof; and in the top grow leaves about the head of
it (the most inmost part whereof they call palmetto,
and it is the heart and pith of the same trunk, so white
and thin as it will peel off into pleats as smooth and
delicate as white satin into twenty folds, in which a man
may write as in paper), where they spread and fall
downward about the tree like an overblown rose or
saffron flower not early gathered. So broad are the
leaves as an Italian umbrella: a man may well defend
his whole body under one of them from the greatest
storm rain that falls; for they being stiff and smooth,
as if so many flags were knit together, the rain easily
slideth off. We oftentimes found growing to these
leaves many silkworms involved therein, like those
small worms which Acosta [39] writeth of, which grew in
the leaves of the tuna[40] tree, of which, being dried, the
Indians make their cochineal, so precious and merchant-
able. With these leaves we thatched our cabins; and,
roasting the palmetto or soft top thereof, they had a
taste like fried melons, and, being sod,[41] they eat like

[39]José de Acosta, *The Natural and Moral History of the East and
West Indies* (1604).

[40]Usually the term for the prickly pear (genus *Opuntia*). Acosta,
after describing the prickly pear, mentions another "tunall" tree bearing worms, probably one of the varieties of cactus on which the scale
insect *Dactylopius coccus* lives.

[41]Stewed.

cabbages, but not so offensively thankful[42] to the stom-
ach. Many an ancient burgher was therefore heaved at
and fell not for his place but for his head. For our
common people, whose bellies never had ears, made it
no breach of charity in their hot bloods and tall stomachs[43] to murder thousands of them. They bear a kind
of berry, black and round, as big as a damson, which
about December were ripe and luscious; being scalded
whilst they are green, they eat like bullaces.[44] These
trees shed their leaves in the winter months, as withered
or burnt with the cold blasts of the north wind, especially those that grow to the seaward; and in March
there burgeon new in their room, fresh and tender.

Other kinds of high and sweet-smelling woods there
be and divers colors, black, yellow, and red, and one
which bears a round blue berry, much eaten by our own
people, of a styptic quality and rough taste on the
tongue like a sloe, to stay or bind the flux, which the
often eating of the luscious palm berry would bring
them into, for the nature of sweet things is to cleanse
and dissolve. A kind of pea of the bigness and shape
of a Catherine pear we found growing upon the rocks,
full of many sharp subtle pricks (as a thistle) which
we therefore called the prickle pear, the outside green,
but, being opened, of a deep murrey, full of juice like

[42]Probably, "flatulent."

[43]Tall stomachs: brave or lusty appetites.

[44]A variety of plum, *Prunus insititia.*

a mulberry and just of the same substance and taste; we both eat them raw and baked.

Sure it is that there are no rivers nor running springs of fresh water to be found upon any of them. When we came first we digged and found certain gushings and soft bubblings, which, being either in bottoms or on the side of hanging ground, were only fed with rain water, which nevertheless soon sinketh into the earth and vanisheth away, or emptieth itself out of sight into the sea, without any channel above or upon the superficies of the earth; for, according as their rains fell, we had our wells and pits (which we digged) either half full or absolute exhausted and dry. Howbeit some low bottoms (which the continual descent from the hills filled full and in those flats could have no passage away) we found to continue, as fishing ponds or standing pools, continually summer and winter full of fresh water.

The shore and bays round about, when we landed first, afforded great store of fish, and that of divers kinds and good, but it should seem that our fires, which we maintained on the shore's side, drave them from us, so as we were in some want until we had made a flat-bottom gondola of cedar, with which we put off farther into the sea and then daily hooked great store of many kinds, as excellent angelfish, salmon peal, bonitos, sting ray, cabally,[45] snappers, hogfish, sharks, dogfish, pil-

[45]Allied to the French *cabillaud* (cod).

chards, mullets, and rockfish, of which be divers kinds. And of these our governor dried and salted and, barreling them up, brought to sea five hundred; for he had procured salt to be made with some brine which happily was preserved, and, once having made a little quantity, he kept three or four pots boiling and two or three men attending nothing else in an house (some little distance from his bay) set up on purpose for the same work.

Likewise in Frobisher's building bay we had a large seine, or trammel net, which our governor caused to be made of the deer toils which we were to carry to Virginia by drawing the masts more strait and narrow with rope yarn, and which reached from one side of the dock to the other, with which (I may boldly say) we have taken five thousand of small and great fish at one hale: as pilchards, breams, mullets, rockfish, etc., and other kinds for which we have no names. We have taken also from under the broken rocks crevises [crayfish] oftentimes greater than any of our best English lobsters, and likewise abundance of crabs, oysters, and whelks. True it is, for fish, in every cove and creek we found snails[46] and skulls[47] in that abundance as I think no island in the world may have greater store or better fish. For they, sucking of the very water which descendeth from the high hills, mingled with juice and verdure of the palms,

[46]The original reads "snaules." Possibly these are sea snails or snailfish.

[47]Skullfish?

cedars, and other sweet woods (which likewise make the herbs, roots, and weeds sweet which grow about the banks), become thereby both fat and wholesome; as must those fish needs be gross, slimy, and corrupt the blood which feed in fens, marshes, ditches, muddy pools, and near unto places where much filth is daily cast forth.

Unscaled fishes, such as Junius[48] calleth *mollis pisces,* as tenches, eel, or lampreys, and such feculent[49] and dangerous snakes, we never saw any, nor may any river be envenomed with them (I pray God) where I come.

I forbear to speak what a sort[50] of whales we have seen hard aboard the shore, followed sometime by the swordfish and the thresher, the sport whereof was not unpleasant, the swordfish with his sharp and needle fin pricking him into the belly, when he would sink and fall into the sea; and when he startled upward from his wounds the thresher with his large fins (like flails) beating him above water. The examples whereof gives us (saith Oviedus) to understand that in the selfsame peril and danger do men live in this mortal life, wherein

[48]Hadrianus Junius, referring to his *Nomenclator octilinguis rerum propria nomine continens.* An English edition was published in 1585, which translates *mollis pisces* as "Soft, smooth, or slippery fishes, without scales."

[49]Impure.

[50]Company; i.e., many.

is no certain security neither in high estate nor low.[51]

Fowl there is great store: small birds, sparrows fat and plump like a bunting, bigger than ours, robins of divers colors, green and yellow, ordinary and familiar in our cabins, and other of less sort. White and gray heronshaws, bitterns, teal, snipes, crows, and hawks, of which in March we found divers aeries, goshawks and tassels,[52] oxbirds, cormorants, bald coots, moor hens, owls, and bats in great store. And upon New Year's Day in the morning, our governor being walked forth with another gentleman, Master James Swift, each of them with their pieces killed a wild swan in a great sea-water bay or pond in our island.

A kind of web-footed fowl[53] there is, of the bigness of an English green plover or sea mew, which all the summer we saw not, and in the darkest nights of November and December (for in the night they only feed) they would come forth but not fly far from home and, hovering in the air and over the sea, made a strange hollo and harsh howling. Their color is inclining to russet, with white bellies (as are likewise the long feathers of their wings russet and white); these gather

[51]This moral is drawn by Oviedo from a contest between flying fish, dolphins, and sea gulls.

[52]Tercels, or male peregrine hawks.

[53]Marginal note: "They call it of the cry which it maketh a cahow." The bird, a variety of shearwater, was so defenseless against the human occupants of the island that it became extinct before many years had passed.

themselves together and breed in those islands, which are high and so far alone[54] into the sea that the wild hogs cannot swim over [to] them, and there in the ground they have their burrows, like conies in a warren and so wrought in the loose mold, though not so deep. Which birds, with a light bough in a dark night (as in our lowbelling[55]), we caught. I have been at the taking of three hundred in an hour, and we might have laden our boats. Our men found a pretty way to take them, which was by standing on the rocks or sands by the seaside and holloing, laughing, and making the strangest outcry that possibly they could. With the noise whereof the birds would come flocking to that place and settle upon the very arms and head of him that so cried, and still creep nearer and nearer, answering the noise themselves; by which our men would weigh them with their hand, and which weighed heaviest they took for the best and let the others alone. And so our men would take twenty dozen in two hours of the chiefest of them; and they were a good and well-relished fowl, fat and full as a partridge. In January we had great

[54]The word possibly should be "along."

[55]A method of fowling at night with sticks, bells, and lights to confuse the birds and drive them into nets. This passage may have suggested to Shakespeare the dialogue between Gonzalo and Sebastian in Act II, scene i, of *The Tempest*:

"*Gon.* . . . You would lift the moon out of her sphere. . . .

Seb. We would so, and then go a-batfowling."

"Batfowling" was another name for "lowbelling."

store of their eggs, which are as great as an hen's egg,
and so fashioned and white shelled, and have no differ-
ence in yolk nor white from an hen's egg. There are
thousands of these birds and two or three islands full
of their burrows, whither at any time (in two hours'
warning) we could send our cockboat and bring home
as many as would serve the whole company. Which
birds for their blindness (for they see weakly in the
day) and for their cry and hooting we called the sea
owl. They will bite cruelly with their crooked bills.

We had knowledge that there were wild hogs upon
the island, at first by our own swine preserved from the
wreck and brought to shore; for they straying into the
woods, an huge wild boar followed down to our quarter,
which at night was watched and taken in this sort. One
of Sir George Somers' men went and lay among the
swine, when, the boar being come and groveled by the
sows, he put over his hand and rubbed the side gently
of the boar, which then lay still; by which means he
fastened a rope with a sliding knot to the hinder leg and
so took him, and after him in this sort two or three
more. But in the end (a little business over) our
people would go a-hunting with our ship dog and sometimes bring home thirty, sometimes fifty boars, sows,
and pigs in a week alive; for the dog would fasten on
them and hold whilst the huntsmen made in. And there
be thousands of them in the islands, and at that time
of the year, in August, September, October, and No-

vember, they were well fed with berries that dropped
from the cedars and the palms; and in our quarter we
made sties for them and, gathering of these berries,
served them twice a day, by which means we kept them
in good plight. And when there was any fret of
weather (for upon every increase of wind the billow
would be so great as it was no putting out with our
gondola or canoe) that we could not fish nor take
tortoises, then we killed our hogs. But in February,
when the palm berries began to be scant or dry, and the
cedar berries failed two months sooner, true it is, the
hogs grew poor; and being taken so, we could not raise
them to be better, for besides those berries we had nothing wherewith to frank[56] them.

But even then the tortoises came in again, of which
we daily both turned up great store, finding them on
land, as also, sculling after them in our boat, stuck
them with an iron goad and sod, baked, and roasted
them. The tortoise is reasonable toothsome (some
say), wholesome meat. I am sure our company liked
the meat of them very well, and one tortoise would go
further amongst them than three hogs. One turtle (for
so we called them) feasted well a dozen messes, ap-
pointing six to every mess. It is such a kind of meat
as a man can neither absolutely call fish nor flesh, keeping mostwhat in the water and feeding upon sea grass
like a heifer in the bottom of the coves and bays, and

[56]Fatten.

laying their eggs (of which we should find five hundred at a time in the opening of a she-turtle) in the sand by the shoreside and so, covering them close, leave them to the hatching of the sun, like the manatee at Santo Domingo, which made the Spanish friars (at their first arrival) make some scruple to eat them on a Friday, because in color and taste the flesh is like to morsels of veal.

Concerning the laying of their eggs and hatching of their young, Peter Martire writeth thus in his *Decades of the Ocean:*

At such time as the heat of nature moveth them to generation, they come forth of the sea, and, making a deep pit in the sand, they lay three or four hundred eggs therein. When they have thus emptied their bag of conception, they put as much of the same again into the pit as may satisfy to cover the eggs and so resort again unto the sea, nothing careful of their succession. At the day appointed of nature to the procreation of these creatures, there creepeth out a multitude of tortoises, as it were pismires out of an anthill, and this only by the heat of the sun, without any help of their parents. Their eggs are as big as geese eggs and themselves, grown to perfection, bigger than great round targets.[57]

[57]The quotation is from Eden or Willes, with some variations in phraseology. This passage actually ends at "geese eggs" in the original; the statement about their size has been added by Strachey from another part of the book.

II

Actions and occurrents while they continued in the islands: Ravens sent for Virginia; divers mutinies; Paine executed; two pinnaces built

---

S O soon as we were a little settled after our landing, with all the conveniency we might and as the place and our many wants would give us leave, we made up our longboat (as Your Ladyship hath heard) in fashion of a pinnace, fitting her with a little deck, made of the hatches of our ruined ship, so close that no water could go in her, gave her sails and oars, and entreating with our master's mate, Henry Ravens (who was supposed a sufficient pilot), we found him easily won to make over therewith as a bark of aviso[58] for Virginia, which, being in the height of 37 degrees, five degrees from the island which we were, might be some 140 leagues from us or thereabouts (reckoning to every degree that lies northeast, and westerly twenty-eight English leagues); who the twenty-eighth of August, being Monday, with six sailors

[58]Bark of aviso: advice boat.

and our cape merchant,[59] Thomas Whittingham, departed from us out of Gates his bay, but to our much wonder returned again upon the Wednesday night after, having attempted to have got clear of the island from the north-northeast to the southwest but could not, as little water as she drew (which might not be above twenty inches), for shoals and breaches. So as he was fain to go out from Somers' Creeks (and the same way we came in) on the south-southeast of the islands, and from thence he made to sea the Friday after, the first of September, promising if he lived and arrived safe there to return unto us the next new moon with the pinnace belonging to the colony there. According unto which instructions were directed unto the new lieutenant governor and council from our governor here, for which the islands were appointed carefully to

[59]Item 22 of "Instructions, Orders, and Constitutions to Sir Thomas Gates, Governor of Virginia," as printed in *The Records of the Virginia Company of London,* edited by Susan Myra Kingsbury (Washington, D. C., 1933), III, 20, reads, in part, as follows: "One officer or two in every fort, whom you must only appoint to be truncmasters [? truckmasters], may dispatch the whole business of trade. . . . And . . . you must by proclamation or edict publicly affixed prohibit and forbid upon pain of punishment of your discretion all other persons to trade or exchange for anything but such as shall be necessary for food or clothing. . . . Over this truncmaster there must be appointed a cape merchant or officer belonging to the store or provision house, that must deliver by book all such things as shall be allowed for trade and receive and take an account of whatsoever is returned, according to the prices therein set, and, so being booked, must store them up to the public use of the colony."

be watched and fires prepared as beacons to have directed and wafted him in. But two moons were wasted upon the promontory before mentioned and gave many a long and wished[60] look round about the horizon, from the northeast to the southwest, but in vain, discovering nothing all the while, which way soever we turned our eye, but air and sea.

You may please, excellent Lady, to know, the reason which moved our governor to dispatch this longboat was the care which he took for the estate of the colony in this his enforced absence. For by a long practiced experience foreseeing and fearing what innovation[61] and tumult might happily[62] arise amongst the younger and ambitious spirits of the new companies to arrive in Virginia, now coming with him along in this same fleet, he framed his letters to the colony and by a particular commission confirmed Captain Peter Wynne his lieutenant governor, with an assistance of six councilors, writing withal to divers and such gentlemen of quality and knowledge of virtue and to such lovers of goodness in this cause whom he knew, entreating them, by giving examples in themselves of duty and obedience, to assist likewise the said lieutenant governor against such as should attempt the innovating of the person (now named by him) or form of government which in some

[60]Hopeful.
[61]Mutiny.
[62]Perhaps.

articles he did likewise prescribe unto them; and [he] had fair hopes all should go well if these his letters might arrive there, until such time as either some ship there (which he fairly believed) might be moved presently to adventure for him, or that it should please the Right Honorable the Lords and the rest of His Majesty's Council in England to address thither the Right Honorable the Lord La Warr (one of more eminency and worthiness), as the project was before his coming forth, whilst by their honorable favors a charitable consideration in like manner might be taken of our estates to redeem us from hence. For which purpose likewise our governor directed a particular letter to the Council in England and sent it to the foresaid Captain Peter Wynne (his now-to-be-chosen lieutenant governor) by him to be dispatched (which is the first) from thence into England.

In his absence Sir George Somers coasted the islands and drew the former plat of them, and daily fished and hunted for our whole company, until the seven-and-twentieth of November, when, then well perceiving that we were not likely to hear from Virginia and conceiving how the pinnace which Richard Frobisher was a-building would not be of burden sufficient to transport all our men from thence into Virginia (especially considering the season of the year wherein we were likely to put off), he consulted with our governor that if he might have two carpenters (for we had four, such as they were) and twenty men over with him into the main island he would quickly frame up another little bark to second ours, for the better fitting and conveyance of our people. Our governor, with many thanks (as the cause required) cherishing this so careful and religious consideration in him (and whose experience likewise was somewhat in these affairs), granted him all things suitable to his desire and to the furthering of the work. Who therefore had made ready for him all such tools and instruments as our own use required not; and for him were drawn forth twenty of the ablest and stoutest of the company and the best of our men to hew and square timber, when himself then, with daily pains and labor, wrought upon a small vessel, which was soon ready as ours. At which we leave him a while busied and return to ourselves.

In the mean space did one Frobisher, born at Gravesend, and at his coming forth now dwelling at Limehouse (a painful and well-experienced shipwright and skillful workman) labor the building of a little pinnace; for the furtherance of which the governor dispensed with no travail of his body nor forbare any care or study of mind, persuading as much and more an ill-qualified parcel of people by his own performance than by authority thereby to hold them at their work, namely to fell, carry, and saw cedar fit for the carpenter's purpose (for what was so mean whereto he would not himself set his hand, being therefor up early and down late?). Yet nevertheless were they hardly drawn to it, as the tortoise to the enchantment, as the proverb is, but his own presence and hand being set to every mean labor and employed so readily to every office made our people at length more diligent and willing to be called thereunto where they should see him before they came. In which we may observe how much example prevails above precepts and how readier men are to be led by eyes than ears.

And sure it was happy for us, who had now run this fortune and were fallen into the bottom of this misery, that we both had our governor with us and one so solicitous and careful whose both example (as I said) and authority could lay shame and command upon our people. Else, I am persuaded, we had most of us finished our days there, so willing were the major part of the common sort (especially when they found such a plenty of victuals) to settle a foundation of ever inhabiting there; as well appeared by many practices of theirs (and perhaps of the better sort). Lo, what are our affections and passions if not rightly squared? How irreligious and irregular they express us! Not perhaps so ill as we would be, but yet as we are. Some dangerous and secret discontents nourished amongst us had like to have been the parents of bloody issues and mischiefs. They began first in the seamen, who in time had fastened unto them (by false baits) many of our landmen likewise, and some of whom (for opinion of their religion) was carried an extraordinary and good respect. The angles wherewith chiefly they thus hooked in these disquieted pools were how that in Virginia nothing but wretchedness and labor must be expected, with many wants and a churlish entreaty,[63] there being neither that fish, flesh, nor fowl which here (without wasting on the one part, or watching on theirs, or any threatening and art of authority) at ease and pleasure might be enjoyed. And since both in the one and the other place they were (for the time) to lose the fruition both of their friends and country, as good and better were it for them to repose and seat them where they should have the least outward wants the while.

This, thus preached and published each to other, though by such who never had been more onward toward Virginia than (before this voyage) a sculler could happily row him (and what hath a more adamantine power to draw unto it the consent and attraction of the idle, untoward,[64] and wretched number of the many than liberty and fullness of sensuality?), begat such a murmur and such a discontent and disunion of hearts and hands from this labor and forwarding the means of redeeming us from hence as each one wrought with his mate how to divorce him from the same.

And first (and it was the first of September) a conspiracy was discovered of which six were found prin-

[63]Churlish entreaty: niggardly provision.
[64]Intractable.

cipals, who had promised each unto the other not to set
their hands to any travail or endeavor which might
expedite or forward this pinnace. And each of these
had severally (according to appointment) sought his
opportunity to draw the smith, and one of our carpenters, Nicholas Bennett, who made much profession of
Scripture, a mutinous and dissembling impostor, the
captain and one of the chief persuaders of others, who
afterward brake from the society of the colony and like
outlaws retired into the woods to make a settlement
and habitation there, on their party, with whom they
purposed to leave our quarter and possess another
island by themselves. But this happily found out, they
were condemned to the same punishment which they
would have chosen (but without smith or carpenter),
and to an island far by itself they were carried and
there left. Their names were John Want, the chief of
them, an Essex man of Newport by Saffron Walden,
both seditious and a sectary in points of religion, in his
own prayers much devout and frequent but hardly
drawn to the public, insomuch as, being suspected by
our minister for a Brownist,[65] he was often compelled
to the common liturgy and form of prayer. The rest
of the confederates were Christopher Carter, Francis
Pearepoint, William Brian, William Martin, Richard
Knowles.

[65] A follower of Robert Browne, an early advocate of the congrega-
tional system of church government.

But soon they missed comfort (who were far removed from our store); besides, the society of their acquaintance had wrought in some of them, if not a loathsomeness of their offense, yet a sorrow that their complement was not more full and therefore a weariness of their being thus untimely prescribed;[66] insomuch as many humble petitions were sent unto our governor, fraught full of their seeming sorrow and repentance and earnest vows to redeem the former trespass, with example of duties[67] in them all to the common cause and general business. Upon which our governor (not easy to admit any accusation and hard to remit an offense, but at all times sorry in the punishment of him in whom may appear either shame or contrition) was easily content to reacknowledge them again.

Yet could not this be any warning to others, who more subtly began to shake the foundation of our quiet safety; and therein did one Stephen Hopkins commence the first act or overture—a fellow who had much knowledge in the Scriptures and could reason well therein, whom our minister therefore chose to be his clerk to read the psalms and chapters upon Sundays at the assembly of the congregation under him; who in January, the twenty-fourth, brake with one Samuel Sharp and Humfrey Reed (who presently discovered it to the governor) and alleged substantial arguments both civil

[66]Outlawed.
[67]Services.

and divine (the Scripture falsely quoted) that it was no
breach of honesty, conscience, nor religion to decline
from the obedience of the governor or refuse to go any
further led by his authority (except it so pleased themselves), since the authority ceased when the wreck was
committed, and, with it, they were all then freed from
the government of any man, and for a matter of conscience it was not unknown to the meanest how much
we were therein bound each one to provide for himself
and his own family. For which were two apparent
reasons to stay them even in this place: first, abundance
by God's providence of all manner of good food; next,
some hope in reasonable time, when they might grow
weary of the place, to build a small bark, with the skill
and help of the aforesaid Nicholas Bennett, whom they
insinuated[68] to them, albeit he was now absent from his
quarter and working in the main island with Sir George
Somers upon his pinnace, to be of the conspiracy, that
so might [they] get clear from hence at their own
pleasures. When in Virginia, the first would be assur-
edly wanting and they might well fear to be detained in
that country by the authority of the commander thereof
and their whole life to serve the turns of the adventurers with their travails and labors.

This being thus laid, and by such a one who had
gotten an opinion (as I before remembered) of re-

[68]Won over by artful persuasion.

ligion, when it was declared by those two accusers, not
knowing what further ground it had or 'complices, it
pleased the governor to let this his factious offense to
have a public affront and contestation by these two
witnesses before the whole company, who (at the toll-
ing of a bell) assembled before a *corps de garde;* where
the prisoner was brought forth in manacles and both
accused and suffered to make at large to every particular his answer, which was only full of sorrow and tears,
pleading simplicity and denial. But he being only found,
at this time, both the captain and the follower of this
mutiny, and generally held worthy to satisfy the punishment of his offense with the sacrifice of his life, our
governor passed the sentence of a martial court upon
him, such as belongs to mutiny and rebellion. But so
penitent he was, and made so much moan, alleging the
ruin of his wife and children in this his trespass, as it
wrought in the hearts of all the better sort of the company, who therefore with humble entreaties and earnest
supplications went unto our governor, whom they be-
sought (as likewise did Captain Newport and myself)
and never left him until we had got his pardon.

In these dangers and devilish disquiets (whilst the
Almighty God wrought for us and sent us, miraculously
delivered from the calamities of the sea, all blessings
upon the shore to content and bind us to gratefulness),
thus enraged amongst ourselves to the destruction each
of other, into what a mischief and misery had we been

given up had we not had a governor with his authority
to have suppressed the same? Yet was there a worse
practice, faction, and conjuration afoot, deadly and
bloody, in which the life of our governor, with many
others, were threatened and could not but miscarry in
his fall. But such is ever the will of God (who in the
execution of His judgments breaketh the firebrands
upon the head of him who first kindleth them), there
were who conceived that our governor indeed neither
durst nor had authority to put in execution or pass the
act of justice upon anyone, how treacherous or impious
soever; their own opinions so much deceiving them for
the unlawfulness of any act which they would execute,
daring to justify among themselves that if they should
be apprehended before the performance they should
happily suffer as martyrs. They persevered, therefore,
not only to draw unto them such a number and asso-
ciates as they could work into the abandoning of our
governor and to the inhabiting of this island: they had
now purposed to have made a surprise of the store-
house and to have forced from thence what was therein
either of meal, cloth, cables, arms, sails, oars, or what
else it pleased God that we had recovered from the
wreck and was to serve our general necessity and use,
either for the relief of us while we stayed here, or for
the carrying of us from this place again when our
pinnace should have been furnished.

But as all giddy and lawless attempts have always

something of imperfection, and that as well by the property of the action, which holdeth of disobedience and rebellion (both full of fear), as through the ignorance of the devisers themselves, so in this (besides those defects) there were some of the association who, not strong enough fortified in their own conceits,[69] brake from the plot itself and (before the time was ripe for the execution thereof) discovered the whole order and every agent and actor thereof; who nevertheless were not suddenly apprehended, by reason the confederates were divided and separated in place, some with us and the chief with Sir George Somers in his island (and indeed all his whole company), but good watch passed upon them, every man from thenceforth commanded to wear his weapon, without which before we freely walked from quarter to quarter and conversed among ourselves, and every man advised to stand upon his guard, his own life not being in safety whilst his next neighbor was not to be trusted.

The sentinels and night-warders doubled, the passages of both the quarters were carefully observed, by which means nothing was further attempted until a gentleman amongst them, one Henry Paine, the thirteenth of March, full of mischief, and every hour preparing something or other, stealing swords, addices, axes, hatchets, saws, augers, planes, mallets, etc., to make good his own bad end, his watch night coming

[69] Conceptions.

about and being called by the captain of the same to be upon the guard, did not only give his said commander evil language but struck at him, doubled his blows, and when he was not suffered to close[70] with him, went off the guard, scoffing at the double diligence and attendance of the watch appointed by the governor, for much[71] purpose, as he said. Upon which, the watch telling him if the governor should understand of this his insolency it might turn him to much blame and happily be as much as his life were worth, the said Paine replied with a settled and bitter violence and in such unreverent terms as I should offend the modest ear too much to express it in his own phrase; but the contents were, how that the governor had no authority of that quality to justify upon anyone (how mean soever in the colony) an action of that nature, and therefore let the governor (said he) kiss, etc. Which words, being with the omitted additions brought the next day unto every common and public discourse, at length they were delivered over to the governor, who, examining well the fact[72] (the transgression so much the more exemplary and odious as being in a dangerous time, in a confederate, and the success of the same wishedly listened after, with a doubtful conceit what might be the issue of so notorious a boldness and impudency), calling

[70]Grapple.
[71]I.e., not much.
[72]Crime.

the said Paine before him and the whole company, where (being soon convinced both by the witness of the commander and many which were upon the watch with him) our governor, who had now the eyes of the whole colony fixed upon him, condemned him to be instantly hanged. And the ladder being ready, after he had made many confessions he earnestly desired, being a gentleman, that he might be shot to death, and toward the evening he had his desire, the sun and his life setting together.

But for the other which were with Sir George, upon the Sunday following (the bark being now in good forwardness and ready to launch in short time from that place, as we supposed, to meet ours at a pond of fresh water where they were both to be moored until such time as, being fully tackled, the wind should serve fair for our putting to sea together), being the eighteenth of March, hearing of Paine's death and fearing he had appeached them and discovered the attempt (who, poor gentleman, therein in so bad a cause was too secret and constant to his own faith engaged unto them, and as little needed as urged thereunto, though somewhat was voluntarily delivered by him), by a mutual consent forsook their labor and Sir George Somers and like outlaws betook them to the wild woods. Whether mere rage and greediness after some little pearl (as it was thought) wherewith they conceived they should forever enrich themselves and saw how to obtain the same easily

in this place, or whether the desire forever to inhabit
here, or what other secret else moved them thereunto,
true it is, they sent an audacious and formal petition to
our governor, subscribed with all their names and seals,
not only entreating him that they might stay here but
(with great art) importuned him that he would perform other conditions with them and not waive nor
evade from some of his own promises, as namely, to
furnish each of them with two suits of apparel and
contribute meal ratably for one whole year, so much
among them as they had weekly now, which was one
pound and an half a week (for such had been our proportion for nine months).

Our governor answered this their petition, writing to
Sir George Somers to this effect: that true it was, at
their first arrival upon this island, when it was feared
how our means would not extend to the making of a
vessel capable and large enough to transport all our
countrymen at once, indeed, out of his Christian consideration (mourning for such his countrymen who,
coming under his command, he foresaw that for a while
he was like enough to leave here behind, compelled by
tyranny of necessity), his purpose was not yet to for-
sake them so, as given up like savages, but to leave
them all things fitting to defend them from want and
wretchedness, as much at least as lay in his power to
spare from the present use (and perhaps necessity of
others, whose fortunes should be to be transported with

him) for one whole year or more (if so long, by any casualty, the ships which he would send unto them might be stayed before their arrival, so many hazards accompanying the sea); but withal entreated Sir George to remember unto his company (if by any means he could learn where they were) how he had vowed unto him that if either his own means, his authority in Virginia, or love with his friends in England could dispatch for them sooner, how far it was from him to let them remain abandoned and neglected without their redemption so long; and then proceeded, requesting Sir George Somers again to signify unto them, since now our own pinnace did arise to that burden and that it would sufficiently transport them all, beside[73] the necessity of any other bark. And yet, that since his bark was now ready too, that those consultations, howsoever charitable and most passionate in themselves, might determine as taken away thereby, and therefore that he should now be pleased to advise them well how unanswerable this grant or consent of his should be: first, to His Majesty for so many of his subjects; next to the adventurers; and lastly, what an imputation and infamy it might be to both their own proper[74] reputations and honors, having each of them authority in their places to compel the adversant and irregular multitude at any time to what should be obedient and honest,

[73]Excluding.
[74]Personal.

which if they should not execute, the blame would not
lie upon the people (at all times wavering and insolent)
but upon themselves, so weak and unworthy in their
command. And moreover entreated him by any secret
practice to apprehend them, since that the obstinate and
precipitate many were no more in such a condition and
state to be favored than the murmuring and mutiny of
such rebellious and turbulent humorists[75] who had not
conscience nor knowledge to draw in the yoke of goodness[76] and in the business for which they were sent out
of England; for which likewise, at the expense and
charge of the adventurers, they were to him committed,
and that the meanest in the whole fleet stood the company in no less than £20 for his own personal transportation and things necessary to accompany him. And
therefore lovingly conjured Sir George, by the worthiness of his (heretofore) well-maintained reputation,
and by the powers of his own judgment, and by the
virtue of that ancient love and friendship which had
these many years been settled between them, to do his
best to give this revolted company (if he could send
unto them) the consideration of these particulars, and
so work with them (if he might) that by fair means
(the mutiny reconciled) they would at length survey
their own errors, which he would be as ready, upon
their rendering and coming in, to pardon, as he did now

[75]Persons who indulge their own changing whims.
[76]Draw in the yoke of goodness: perform their duty submissively.

pity them; assuring them in general and particular that whatsoever they had sinisterly committed or practiced hitherto against the laws of duty and honesty should not in any sort be imputed against them.

In which good office Sir George Somers did so nobly work and heartily labor as he brought most of them in, and indeed all but Christopher Carter and Robert Waters, who by no means would any more come amongst Sir George's men, hearing that Sir George had commanded his men (since they would not be entreated by fair means) to surprise them if they could by any device or force. From which time they grew so cautelous[77] and wary for their own ill as at our coming away we were fain to leave them behind. That Waters was a sailor, who at his first landing upon the island (as after you shall hear) killed another fellow sailor of his, the body of the murdered and murderer so dwelling, as prescribed, now together.

During our time of abode upon these islands we had daily every Sunday two sermons preached by our minister; besides every morning and evening at the ringing of a bell we repaired all to public prayer, at what time the names of our whole company were called by bill, and such as were wanting were duly punished.

The contents (for the most part) of all our preacher's sermons were especially of thankfulness and unity, etc.

[77]Crafty.

It pleased God also to give us opportunity to perform all the other offices and rites of our Christian profession in this island: as marriage, for the six-and-twentieth of November we had one of Sir George Somers his men, his cook named Thomas Powell, who married a maidservant of one Mistress Horton, whose name was Elizabeth Persons; and upon Christmas Eve, as also once before, the first of October, our minister preached a godly sermon, which being ended he celebrated a Communion, at the partaking whereof our governor was and the greatest part of our company; and the eleventh of February we had the child of one John Rose[78] christened, a daughter, to which Captain Newport and myself were witnesses and the aforesaid Mistress Horton, and we named it Bermuda; as also, the five-and-twentieth of March, the wife of one Edward Eason, being delivered the week before of a boy, had him then christened, to which Captain Newport and myself and Master James Swift were godfathers, and we named it Bermudas.

Likewise, we buried five of our company: Jeffery Briars, Richard Lewis, William Hitchman, and my goddaughter, Bermuda Rolfe, and one untimely Edward Samuel, a sailor, being villainously killed by the foresaid Robert Waters (a sailor likewise) with a shovel, who strake him therewith under the lift of the ear; for which he was apprehended and appointed to

[78]I.e., John Rolfe, who later married Pocahontas.

be hanged the next day (the fact being done in the twilight). But being bound fast to a tree all night, with many ropes and a guard of five or six to attend him, his fellow sailors (watching the advantage of the sentinels' sleeping), in despite and disdain that justice should be showed upon a sailor and that one of their crew should be an example to others, not taking into consideration the unmanliness of the murder nor the horror of the sin, they cut his bonds and conveyed him into the woods, where they fed him nightly and closely, who afterward by the mediation of Sir George Somers, upon many conditions, had his trial respited by our governor.

We had brought our pinnace so forward by this time as, the eight-and-twentieth of August we having laid her keel, the six-and-twentieth of February we now began to calk. Old cables we had preserved unto us, which afforded oakum enough; and one barrel of pitch and another of tar we likewise saved, which served our use some little way upon the bilge. We breamed[79] her otherwise with lime made of whelk shells and an hard white stone which we burned in a kiln, slaked with fresh water and tempered with tortoises' oil. The thirtieth of March, being Friday, we towed her out in the morning spring tide from the wharf where she was built, buoying her with four casks in her run only, which opened into the northwest and into which, when the breeze stood north and by west with any stiff gale and upon the

[79]Cleaned her bottom.

spring tides, the sea would increase with that violence, especially twice it did so, as at the first time (before our governor had caused a solid causeway of an hundred load of stone to be brought from the hills and neighbor rocks and round about her ribs from stem to stem, where it made a pointed balk and thereby brake the violence of the flow and billow) it endangered her overthrow and ruin, being green, as it were, upon the stocks. With much difficulty, diligence, and labor we saved her at the first, all her bases, shores, and piles which underset her being almost carried from her; which was the second of January, when her knees were not set to nor one joint firm.

We launched her unrigged, to carry her to a little round island lying west-northwest and close aboard to the back side of our island, both nearer the ponds and wells of some fresh water, as also from thence to make our way to the sea the better, the channel being there sufficient and deep enough to lead her forth when her masts, sails, and all her trim should be about her. She was forty foot by the keel and nineteen foot broad at the beam, six-foot floor; her rake forward was fourteen foot, her rake aft from the top of her post (which was twelve foot long) was three foot; she was eight foot deep under her beam; between her decks she was four foot and an half, with a rising of half a foot more under her forecastle, of purpose to scour the deck with small shot if at any time we should be boarded by the enemy. She had a fall of eighteen inches aft, to make her steerage and her great cabin the more large; her steerage was five foot long and six foot high, with a close gallery right aft, with a window on each side and two right aft. The most part of her timber was cedar, which we found to be bad for shipping for that it is wondrous false inward, and besides it is so spalled or brickle[80] that it will make no good planks; her beams were all oak of our ruined ship, and some planks in her bow of oak, and the rest as is afore said. When she began to swim (upon her launching) our governor called her the "Deliverance," and she might be some eighty tons of burden.

Before we quitted our old quarter and dislodged to the fresh water with our pinnace, our governor set up in Sir George Somers' garden a fair mnemosynon[81] in figure of a cross, made of some of the timber of our ruined ship, which was screwed in with strong and great trunnels to a mighty cedar, which grew in the midst of the said garden and whose top and upper branches he caused to be lopped, that the violence of the wind and weather might have the less power over her. In the midst of the cross, our governor fastened the picture of His Majesty in a piece of silver of twelvepence, and on each side of the cross he set an inscription graven in copper in the Latin and English to this purpose:

[80]Brittle.
[81]Memorial.

In memory of our great deliverance, both from a mighty storm and leak, we have set up this to the honor of God. It is the spoil of an English ship (of three hundred ton) called the "Sea Venture," bound with seven ships more (from which the storm divided us) to Virginia, or Nova Britannia, in America. In it were two knights, Sir Thomas Gates, Knight, governor of the English forces and colony there, and Sir George Somers, Knight, admiral of the seas. Her captain was Christopher Newport; passengers and mariners she had beside (which came all safe to land) one hundred and fifty. We were forced to run her ashore (by reason of her leak) under a point that bore southeast from the northern point of the island, which we discovered first the eight-and-twentieth of July, 1609.

About the last of April, Sir George Somers launched his pinnace and brought her from his building bay in the main island into the channel where ours did ride; and she was by the keel nine-and-twenty foot, at the beam fifteen foot and an half, at the luff fourteen, at the transom nine; and she was eight foot deep and drew six foot water, and he called her the "Patience."

III

*Their departure from Bermuda and arrival in Vir-
ginia: miseries there, departure and return upon the
Lord La Warr's arriving; Jamestown described*

ROM this time we only awaited a favorable westerly wind to carry us forth,
which longer than usual now kept at
the east and southeast, the way which
we were to go. The tenth of May early,
Sir George Somers and Captain Newport went off
with their longboats and with two canoes buoyed the
channel which we were to lead it out in and which was
no broader from shoals on the one side and rocks on
the other than about three times the length of our
pinnace. About ten of the clock, that day being Thursday, we set sail an easy gale, the wind at south, and by
reason no more wind blew we were fain to tow her with
our longboat; yet neither with the help of that were we
able to fit our buoys, but even when we came just upon
them we struck a rock on the starboard side, over which
the buoy rid, and had it not been a soft rock, by which
means she bore it before her and crushed it to pieces,

God knows we might have been like enough to have returned anew and dwelt there, after ten months of carefulness and great labor, a longer time; but God was more merciful unto us. When she struck upon the rock, the coxswain, one Walsingham, being in the boat with a quick spirit[82] (when we were all amazed[83] and our hearts failed), and so by God's goodness we led it out at three fathom and three fathom and an half water.

The wind served us easily all that day and the next, when (God be ever praised for it), to the no little joy of us all, we got clear of the islands. After which, holding a southerly course, for seven days we had the wind sometimes fair and sometimes scarce and contrary; in which time we lost Sir George Somers twice, albeit we still spared him our main topsail and sometimes our forecourse too.

The seventeenth of May we saw change of water and had much rubbish swim by our ship side, whereby we knew we were not far from land. The eighteenth about midnight we sounded with the dipsey lead and found thirty-seven fathom. The nineteenth in the morning we sounded and had nineteen and an half fathom, stony and sandy ground. The twentieth about midnight we had a marvelous sweet smell from the shore (as from the coast of Spain short of the Straits), strong and pleasant, which did not a little glad us. In the

[82]A word or words may be omitted here.
[83]Overcome with dismay.

morning by daybreak (so soon as one might well see
from the foretop) one of the sailors descried land;
about an hour after I went up and might discover two
hummocks to the southward, from which (northward
all along) lay the land which we were to coast to Cape
Henry. About seven of the clock we cast forth an
anchor, because the tide (by reason of the freshet that
set into the bay) made a strong ebb there and the wind
was but easy, so as, not being able to stem the tide, we
purposed to lie at an anchor until the next flood; but
the wind coming southwest a loom[84] gale about eleven,
we set sail again and, having got over the bar, bore in
for the Cape.

This is the famous Chesapeake Bay, which we have
called (in honor of our young Prince) Cape Henry,
over against which within the Bay lieth another head-
land, which we called, in honor of our princely Duke
of York, Cape Charles; and these lie northeast and by
east and southwest and by west, and they may be distant
each from the other in breadth seven leagues, between
which the sea runs in as broad as between Queen-
borough and Leigh.[85] Indeed it is a goodly bay and a
fairer not easily to be found.

The one-and-twentieth, being Monday in the morning, we came up within two miles of Point Comfort,
when the captain of the fort discharged a warning piece

[84]Gentle.
[85]Queenborough in Kent and Leigh in Essex.

at us, whereupon we came to an anchor and sent off our longboat to the fort to certify who we were. By reason of the shoals which lie on the south side, this fort easily commands the mouth of the river, albeit it is as broad as between Greenwich and the Isle of Dogs.

True it is, such who talked with our men from the shore delivered how safely all our ships the last year (excepting only the admiral and the little pinnace, in which one Michael Philes commanded, of some twenty ton, which we towed astern till the storm blew) arrived, and how our people (well increased) had therefore builded this fort; only we could not learn anything of our longboat sent from the Bermudas but what we gathered by the Indians themselves, especially from Powhatan, who would tell our men of such a boat landed in one of his rivers and would describe the people and make much scoffing sport thereat: by which we have gathered that it is most likely how it arrived upon our coast and, not meeting with our river, were taken at some time or other at some advantage by the savages and so cut off. When our skiff came up again the good news of our ships' and men's arrival the last year did not a little glad our governor, who went soon ashore and as soon (contrary to all our fair hopes) had new, unexpected, uncomfortable, and heavy news of a worse condition of our people above at Jamestown.

Upon Point Comfort our men did the last year (as you have heard) raise a little fortification, which since hath been better perfected and is likely to prove a strong fort and is now kept by Captain James Davies with forty men, and hath to name Algernon Fort, so called by Captain George Percy, whom we found at our arrival president of the colony and at this time likewise in the fort when we got into the Point, which was the one-and-twentieth of May, being Monday about noon; where, riding before an Indian town called Kecoughtan,[86] a mighty storm of thunder, lightning, and rain gave us a shrewd[87] and fearful welcome.

From hence in two days (only by the help of tides, no wind stirring) we plied it sadly up the river, and the three-and-twentieth of May we cast anchor before Jamestown, where we landed, and our much grieved governor, first visiting the church, caused the bell to be rung, at which all such as were able to come forth of their houses repaired to church, where our minister, Master Bucke, made a zealous and sorrowful prayer, finding all things so contrary to our expectations, so full of misery and misgovernment.

After service our governor caused me to read his commission and Captain Percy (then president) delivered up unto him his commission, the old patent, and the council seal. Viewing the fort, we found the palisades torn down, the ports open, the gates from off the hinges, and empty houses (which owners' death had

[86]The modern Hampton, Virginia.
[87]Sharp; distressing.

taken from them) rent up and burnt, rather than the
dwellers would step into the woods a stone's cast off
from them to fetch other firewood. And it is true, the
Indian killed as fast without, if our men stirred but
beyond the bounds of their blockhouse, as famine and
pestilence did within; with many more particularities of
their sufferances (brought upon them by their own dis-
orders the last year) than I have heart to express.

In this desolation and misery our governor found the
condition and state of the colony and (which added
more to his grief) no hope how to amend it or save his
own company and those yet remaining alive from falling into the like necessities. For we had brought from
the Bermudas no greater store of provision (fearing no
such accidents possible to befall the colony here) than
might well serve 150 for a sea voyage. And it was not
possible at this time of the year to amend it by any help
from the Indian; for besides that they (at their best)
have little more than from hand to mouth, it was now
likewise but their seedtime and all their corn scarce put
into the ground. Nor was there at the fort (as they
whom we found related unto us) any means to take fish,
neither sufficient seine nor other convenient net, and yet
if there had, there was not one eye of sturgeon yet come
into the river. All which considered, it pleased our
governor to make a speech unto the company, giving
them to understand that what provision he had they
should equally share with him, and if he should find it

not possible and easy to supply them with something
from the country by the endeavors of his able men, he
would make ready and transport them all into their
native country (accommodating them the best that he
could) ; at which there was a general acclamation and
shout of joy on both sides, for even our own men began
to be disheartened and faint when they saw this misery
amongst the others and no less threatened unto themselves. In the meanwhile, our governor published certain orders and instructions which he enjoined them
strictly to observe, the time that he should stay amongst
them, which, being written out fair, were set up upon a
post in the church for everyone to take notice of.

If I should be examined from whence and by what
occasion all these disasters and afflictions descended
upon our people, I can only refer you (honored Lady)
to the book which the adventurers have sent hither entitled *Advertisements unto the Colony in Virginia*,[88]
wherein the ground and causes are favorably abridged
from whence these miserable effects have been pro-
duced; not excusing likewise the form of government
of some error, which was not powerful enough among
so heady a multitude, especially, as those who arrived

[88]No such printed book is known to exist. Alexander Brown suggested in *The Genesis of the United States* (Boston and New York,
1890), I, 417, that the title in question might be *A True and Sincere
Declaration of the Purpose and Ends of the Plantation* (London, 1610),
which is a different work from the *True Declaration* quoted at the end
of this narrative.

here in the supply sent the last year with us, with whom
the better authority and government, now changed into
an absolute command, came along and had been as
happily established, had it pleased God that we with
them had reached our wished harbor.

Unto such calamity can sloth, riot, and vanity bring
the most settled and plentiful estate. Indeed (right
noble Lady) no story can remember unto us more woes
and anguishes than these people, thus governed, have
both suffered and pulled upon their own heads. And
yet, true it is, some of them, whose voices and command
might not be heard, may easily be absolved from the
guilt hereof, as standing untouched and upright in their
innocencies; whilst the privy factionaries shall never
find time nor darkness to wipe away or cover their
ignoble and irreligious practices, who, it may be, lay all
the discredits and imputations the while upon the country. But under pardon, let me speak freely to them:
let them remember that if riot and sloth should both
meet in any one of their best families in a country most
stored with abundance and plenty in England — continual wasting, no husbandry, the old store still spent
on, no order for new provisions — what better could
befall unto the inhabitants, landlords, and tenants of
that corner than, necessarily following, cleanness of
teeth, famine, and death? Is it not the sentence and
doom of the wise man? "Yet a little sleep, a little
slumber, and a little folding of the hands to sleep: so
thy poverty cometh, as one that travaileth by the way,

and thy necessity like an armed man."[89] And with this
idleness, when something was in store, all wasteful
courses exercised to the heighth, and the headless multitude (some neither of quality nor religion) not employed to the end for which they were sent hither—no,
not compelled (since in themselves unwilling) to sow
corn for their own bellies, nor to put a root, herb, etc.,
for their own particular good in their gardens or elsewhere—I say, in this neglect and sensual surfeit, all
things suffered to run on, to lie sick and languish, must
it be expected that health, plenty, and all the goodness
of a well-ordered state, of necessity for all this, to flow
in this country? You have a right and noble heart
(worthy Lady), be judge of the truth herein.

Then suffer it not be concluded unto you, nor believe,
I beseech you, that the wants and wretchedness which
they have endured ascend out of the poverty and vile-
ness of the country, whether be respected the land or
rivers; the one and the other having not only promised
but poured enough in their veins to convince them[90] in
such calumnies and to quit [91] those common calamities
which (as the shadow accompanies the body) the pre-
cedent neglects touched at, if truly followed and
wrought upon. What England may boast of, having

[89]Prov. 6:10-11.

[90]Convince them: convict them (the slanderers of the country) of
guilt.

[91]Requite; offset.

the fair hand of husbandry to manure and dress it, God
and nature have favorably bestowed upon this country;
and as it hath given unto it, both by situation, height,
and soil, all those (past hopes) assurances which follow
our well-planted native country and others lying under
the same influence, if, as ours, the country and soil
might be improved and drawn forth, so hath it endowed
it, as is most certain, with many more, which England
fetcheth far unto her from elsewhere. For, first, we
have experience, and even our eyes witness (how young
soever we are to the country), that no country yieldeth
goodlier corn nor more manifold increase. Large fields
we have, as prospects of the same, and not far from our
palisade. Besides, we have thousands of goodly vines
in every hedge and bosk, running along the ground,
which yield a plentiful grape in their kind. Let me ap-
peal, then, to knowledge, if these natural vines were
planted, dressed, and ordered by skillful *vignerons,*
whether we might not make a perfect grape and fruitful
vintage in short time. And we have made trial of our
own English seeds, kitchen herbs, and roots and find
them to prosper as speedily as in England.

Only let me truly acknowledge, they are not an
hundred or two of debauched hands, dropped forth by
year after year, with penury and leisure, ill provided
for before they come and worse to be governed when
they are here—men of such distempered bodies and
infected minds, whom no examples daily before their

eyes, either of goodness or punishment, can deter from their habitual impieties or terrify from a shameful death — that must be the carpenters and workmen in this so glorious a building.

Then let no rumor of the poverty of the country (as if in the womb thereof there lay not those elemental seeds which could produce as many fair births of plenty and increase and better hopes than any land under the heaven to which the sun is no nearer a neighbor), I say, let no imposture rumor, nor any fame of some one or a few more changeable actions interposing by the way or at home, waive any man's fair purposes hitherward or wrest them to a declining and falling-off from the business.

I will acknowledge, dear Lady, I have seen much propenseness[92] already toward the unity and general endeavors. How contentedly do such as labor with us go forth when men of rank and quality assist and set on their labors! I have seen it and I protest it, I have heard the inferior people with alacrity of spirit profess that they should never refuse to do their best in the practice of their sciences and knowledges when such worthy and noble gentlemen go in and out before them, and not only so but, as the occasion shall be offered, no less help them with their hand than defend them with the sword. And it is to be understood that such as labor are not yet so taxed but that easily they perform

[92]Inclination.

the same and ever by ten of the clock have done their
morning's work: at what time they have their allowances set out ready for them, and until it be three of the
clock again they take their own pleasure, and afterward, with the sunset, their day's labor is finished. In
all which courses if the business be continued, I doubt
nothing, with God's favor toward us, but to see it in
time a country, an haven, and a staple[93] fitted for such
a trade as shall advance assureder increase, both to the
adventurers and free burghers thereof, than any trade
in Christendom, or than that (even in her early days,
when Michael Cavacco,[94] the Greek, did first discover
it to our English factor in Poland) which extends itself
now from Calpe[95] and Abila,[96] to the bottom of Sidon
and so wide as Alexandria, and all the ports and havens
north and south through the arches[97] to Chios, Smyrna,
Troy, the Hellespont, and up to Pompey's Pillar,[98]
which as a pharos, or watchtower, stands upon the
wondrous opening into the Euxine[99] Sea.

From the three-and-twentieth of May unto the
seventh of June our governor attempted and made trial

[93]Commercial center.

[94]No information about this incident has been found. Perhaps
Strachey heard of it when he was in the Levant with Thomas Glover.

[95]The ancient name for the Rock of Gibraltar.

[96]Jebel Musa, one of the Pillars of Hercules.

[97]The Greek Archipelago.

[98]A column attributed to Pompey the Great, as was the one at
Alexandria.

[99]Black.

of all the ways that both his own judgment could
prompt him in and the advice of Captain George Percy
and those gentlemen whom he found of the council
when he came in, as of others whom he caused to deliver their knowledges concerning the state and condition of the country. But after much debating it could
not appear how possibly they might preserve themselves
(reserving that little which we brought from the Bermudas in our ships and was upon all occasions to stand
good by us) ten days from starving. For besides that
the Indians were of themselves poor, they were forbidden likewise (by their subtle King Powhatan) at all
to trade with us; and not only so, but to endanger and
assault any boat upon the river or straggler out of the
fort by land, by which (not long before our arrival)
our people had a large boat cut off and divers of our
men killed, even within command of our blockhouse; as,
likewise, they shot two of our people to death after we
had been four and five days come in. And yet would
they dare then to enter our ports and truck with us (as
they counterfeited underhand) when, indeed, they came
but as spies to discover our strength, trucking with us
upon such hard conditions that our governor might very
well see their subtlety and therefore neither could well
endure nor would continue it. And I may truly say beside, so had our men abased and to such a contempt had
they brought the value of our copper that a piece which
would have bought a bushel of their corn in former

time would not now buy a little cade or basket of a
pottle.[100] And for this misgovernment chiefly our
colony is much bound to the mariners, who never yet in
any voyage hither but have made a prey of our poor
people in want; insomuch as unless they might advance
four or five for one (how assured soever of the pay-
ments of their bills of exchange) they would not spare
them a dust[101] of corn nor a pint of beer to give unto
them the least comfort or relief, although that beer
purloined and stolen perhaps, either from some particular supply or from the general store: so uncharitable
a parcel of people they be and ill conditioned.

I myself have heard the master of a ship say (even
upon the arrival of this fleet with the lord governor and
captain general, when the said master was treated with
for such commodities as he brought to sell) that unless
he might have an East Indian increase, four for one,
all charges cleared, he would not part with a can of
beer. Besides, to do us more villainy and mischief, they
would send of their longboats still by night and (well
guarded) make out to the neighbor villages and towns
and there (contrary to the articles of the fort, which
now pronounce death for a trespass of that quality)
truck with the Indians, giving for their trifles, otter
skins, beavers, raccoon furs, bears' skins, etc., so large
a quantity and measure of copper as, when the truck-

[100]A measure equivalent to half a gallon.
[101]Grain.

master for the colony in the daytime offered trade, the Indians would laugh and scorn the same, telling what bargains they met withal by night from our *mangot quintans* (so calling our great ships); by which means, the market with them forestalled thus by these dishonest men, I may boldly say they have been a consequent cause (this last year) to the death and starving of many a worthy spirit.

But I hope to see a true amendment and reformation, as well of those as of divers other intolerable abuses thrust upon the colony by these shameless people; as also, for the transportation of such provisions and supplies as are sent hither and come under the charge of pursers (a parcel, fragment, and odd ends of fellows, dependencies to the others), a better course thought upon, of which supplies never yet came into the store or to the parties unto whom such supplies were sent, by relation hitherto, a moiety or third part: for the speedy redress of this, being so sovereign a point, I understand how the lord governor and captain general hath advised unto the council that there may be no more provisions at all delivered unto pursers, but hath entreated to have the provision thus ordered. He would have a commissary general of the victuals to be appointed, who (receiving the store for the colony, by indenture from the treasurer and victualers in England) may keep a just accompt what the gross amounteth unto and what is transported every voyage, in several kinds, as of bread, meat, beer, wine, etc., which said commissary shall deliver over the same to the master of every ship and take an indenture from the said master of what he hath in charge and what he is to deliver to the treasurer of the store in Virginia: of which, if any be wanting, he the said master shall make it good out of his own entertainment;[102] otherwise the pursers, stewards, coopers, and quartermasters will be sure still, not only to give themselves and their friends double allowances, but think it all well gotten that they can purloin and steal away.

Besides that the Indian thus evil entreated us, the river (which were wont before this time of the year to be plentiful of sturgeon) had not now a fish to be seen in it, and albeit we labored and hauled our net twenty times, day and night, yet we took not so much as would content half the fishermen. Our governor therefore sent away his longboat to coast the river downward as far as Point Comfort and from thence to Cape Henry and Cape Charles and all within the Bay; which, after a sevennight's trial and travail, returned without any fruits of their labors, scarce getting so much fish as served their own company.

And to take anything from the Indian by force we never used, nor willingly ever will. And though they had well deserved it, yet it was not now time, for they did (as I said before) but then set their corn, and at

[102]Provision.

their best they had but from hand to mouth. So as
what now remained? Such as we found in the fort, had
we stayed but four days, had doubtless been the most
part of them starved, for their best relief was only
mushrooms and some herbs which, sod together, made
but a thin and unsavory broth and swelled them much.
The pity hereof moved our governor to draw forth
such provision as he had brought, proportioning a
measure equally to every one alike. But then our governor began to examine how long this his store would
hold out and found it (husbanded to the best advantage) not possible to serve longer than sixteen days,
after which nothing was to be possibly supposed out of
the country (as before remembered), nor remained
there then any means to transport him elsewhere.
Whereupon he then entered into the consultation with
Sir George Somers and Captain Newport, calling unto
the same the gentlemen and council of the former government, entreating both the one and the other to advise with him what was best to be done.

The provision which they both had aboard himself
and Sir George Somers was examined and delivered,
how it, being racked to the uttermost, extended not
above, as I said, sixteen days, after[103] two cakes a day.
The gentlemen of the town, who knew better of the
country, could not give him any hope or ways how to
improve it from the Indian. It soon, then, appeared

[103] Apportioned at the rate of.

most fit, by a general approbation, that to preserve and save all from starving there could be no readier course thought on than to abandon the country and, accommodating themselves the best that they might in the present pinnaces then in the road, namely, in the "Discovery" and the "Virginia" and in the two brought from and builded at the Bermudas, the "Deliverance" and the "Patience," with all speed convenient to make for the Newfoundland, where (being the fishing time) they might meet with many English ships into which happily they might disperse most of the company.

This consultation taking effect, our governor, having caused to be carried aboard all the arms and all the best things in the store which might to the adventurers make some commodity upon the sale thereof at home, and burying our ordnances before the fort gate which looked into the river, the seventh of June, having appointed to every pinnace, likewise, his complement and number, also delivered thereunto a proportionable rate of provision, he commanded every man at the beating of the drum to repair aboard. And because he would preserve the town (albeit now to be quitted) unburned, which some intemperate and malicious people threatened, his own company he caused to be last ashore and was himself the last of them when about noon, giving a farewell with a peal of small shot, we set sail and that night, with the tide, fell down to an island in the river, which our people have called Hog Island; and the

morning tide brought us to another island, which we
have called Mulberry Island, where, lying at an anchor
in the afternoon stemming the tide, we discovered a
longboat making toward us from Point Comfort. Much
descant we made thereof![104]   About an hour it came up,
by which, to our no little joys, we had intelligence of
the Honorable My Lord La Warr his arrival before
Algernon Fort the sixth of June, at what time, true it
is, His Lordship, having understood of our governor's
resolution to depart the country, with all expedition
caused his skiff to be manned and in it dispatched his
letters by Captain Edward Bruster (who commandeth
His Lordship's company) to our governor, which pre-
venting[105] us before the aforesaid Mulberry Island (the
eighth of June afore said), upon the receipt of His
Honor's letters, our governor bore up the helm with
the wind coming easterly and that night (the wind so
favorable) relanded all his men at the fort again.
Before which (the tenth of June, being Sunday) His
Lordship had likewise brought his ships and in the
afternoon came ashore with Sir Ferdinando Wainman
and all His Lordship's followers.

Here (worthy Lady) let me have a little your pardon, for, having now a better heart than when I first
landed, I will briefly describe unto you the situation and

[104]I.e., they made many conjectures as to the meaning of the boat's
appearance.
[105]Forestalling.

form of our fort. When Captain Newport in his first
voyage did not like to inhabit upon so open a road as
Cape Henry nor Point Comfort, he plied it up to the
river, still looking out for the most apt and securest
place, as well for his company to sit down in as which
might give the least cause of offense or distaste, in his
judgment, to the inhabitants. At length, after much and
weary search (with their barge coasting still before, as
Vergil writeth Aeneas did, arriving in the region of
Italy called Latium, upon the banks of the river Tiber)
in the country of a werowance called Wowinchapuncke
(a ditionary[106] to Powhatan), within this fair river of
Paspahegh, which we have called the King's River,[107]
a country least inhabited by the Indian, as they all the
way observed, and threescore miles and better up the
fresh channel from Cape Henry, they had sight of an
extended plain and spot of earth which thrust out into
the depth and midst of the channel, making a kind of
chersonese or peninsula, for it was fastened only to the
land with a slender neck no broader than a man may
well quoit a tile shard, and no inhabitants by seven or
six miles near it. The trumpets sounding, the admiral
struck sail, and before the same the rest of the fleet
came to an anchor, and here (as the best yet offered
unto their view, supposed so much the more convenient
by how much with their small company they were like

[106]Subject.
[107]The James.

enough the better to assure it), to lose no further time,
the colony disembarked and every man brought his particular store and furniture, together with the general
provision, ashore. For the safety of which, as likewise
for their own security, ease, and better accommodating,
a certain canton and quantity of that little half island
of ground was measured, which they began to fortify
and thereon in the name of God to raise a fortress with
the ablest and speediest means they could; which fort,
growing since to more perfection, is now at this present
in this manner.

A low level of ground about half an acre (or so
much as Queen Dido might buy of King Iarbas, which
she compassed about with the thongs cut out of one bull
hide and therein built her castle of Byrsa) on the north
side of the river is cast almost into the form of a
triangle and so palisaded. The south side next the river
(howbeit extended in a line or curtain sixscore foot
more in length than the other two, by reason the advantage of the ground doth so require) contains 140
yards, the west and east sides a hundred only. At every
angle or corner, where the lines meet, a bulwark or
watchtower is raised and in each bulwark a piece of
ordnance or two well mounted. To every side, a pro-
portioned distance from the palisade, is a settled street
of houses that runs along, so as each line of the angle
hath his street. In the midst is a market place, a store-
house, and a *corps de garde,* as likewise a pretty chapel,

though (at this time when we came in) as ruined and
unfrequented. But the lord governor and captain general hath given order for the repairing of it, and at this
instant many hands are about it. It is in length three-
score foot, in breadth twenty-four, and shall have a
chancel in it of cedar and a communion table of the
black walnut, and all the pews of cedar, with fair broad
windows to shut and open, as the weather shall occasion, of the same wood, a pulpit of the same, with a
font hewn hollow, like a canoe, with two bells at the
west end. It is so cast as it be very light within, and
the lord governor and captain general doth cause it to
be kept passing sweet and trimmed up with divers
flowers, with a sexton belonging to it. And in it every
Sunday we have sermons twice a day, and every Thursday a sermon, having true preachers, which take their
weekly turns; and every morning, at the ringing of a
bell about ten of the clock, each man addresseth himself
to prayers, and so at four of the clock before supper.

Every Sunday, when the lord governor and captain
general goeth to church, he is accompanied with all the
councilors, captains, other officers, and all the gentlemen, and with a guard of halberdiers in His Lordship's
livery, fair red cloaks, to the number of fifty, both on
each side and behind him; and, being in the church, His
Lordship hath his seat in the choir, in a green velvet
chair, with a cloth, with a velvet cushion spread on a
table before him on which he kneeleth; and on each side

sit the council, captains, and officers, each in their place;
and when he returneth home again he is waited on to
his house in the same manner.

And thus enclosed, as I said, round with a palisade of
planks and strong posts, four foot deep in the ground,
of young oaks, walnuts, etc., the fort is called, in honor
of His Majesty's name, Jamestown. The principal gate
from the town, through the palisade, opens to the river,
as at each bulwark there is a gate likewise to go forth
and at every gate a demiculverin,[108] and so in the market place. The houses first raised were all burnt by a
casualty of fire the beginning of the second year of their
seat and in the second voyage of Captain Newport,
which since have been better rebuilded, though as yet in
no great uniformity, either for the fashion or beauty of
the street. A delicate wrought fine kind of mat the
Indians make, with which (as they can be trucked for
or snatched up) our people do dress their chambers and
inward rooms, which make their houses so much the
more handsome. The houses have wide and large
country chimneys, in the which is to be supposed (in
such plenty of wood) what fires are maintained; and
they have found the way to cover their houses now (as
the Indians) with barks of trees, as durable and as good
proof against storms and winter weather as the best
tile, defending likewise the piercing sunbeams of summer and keeping the inner lodgings cool enough, which

108A small cannon.

before in sultry weather would be like stoves, whilst they were, as at first, pargeted and plastered with bitumen or tough clay. And thus armed for the injury of changing times and seasons of the year we hold ourselves well apaid,[109] though wanting arras[110] hangings, tapestry, and gilded Venetian cordovan, or more spruce household garniture and wanton city ornaments, remembering the old epigraph:

> We dwell not here to build us bowers
> And halls for pleasure and good cheer:
> But halls we build for us and ours,
> To dwell in them whilst we live here.

True it is, I may not excuse this our fort, or Jamestown, as yet seated in somewhat an unwholesome and sickly air, by reason it is in a marish[111] ground, low, flat to the river, and hath no fresh-water springs serving the town but what we drew from a well six or seven fathom deep, fed by the brackish river oozing into it; from whence I verily believe the chief causes have proceeded of many diseases and sicknesses which have happened to our people, who are indeed strangely afflicted with fluxes and agues, and every particular[112] infirmity too: all which, if it had been our fortunes to have seated

[109]Satisfied.

[110]Originally tapestry from Arras, but later applied to painted cloth hangings, which is apparently what Strachey means.

[111]Marshy.

[112]Peculiar to individual constitutions.

upon some hill, accommodated with fresh springs and clear air, as do the natives of the country, we might have, I believe, well escaped. And some experience we have to persuade ourselves that it may be so, for of four hundred and odd men which were seated at the Falls the last year when the fleet came in with fresh and young able spirits under the government of Captain Francis West, and of one hundred to the seawards (on the south side of our river), in the country of the Nansemonds, under the charge of Captain John Martin, there did not so much as one man miscarry and but few or none fall sick; whereas at Jamestown, the same time and the same months, one hundred sickened and half the number died.[113] Howbeit, as we condemn not Kent in England for a small town called Plumstead, continually assaulting the dwellers there (especially newcomers) with agues and fever, no more let us lay scandal and imputation upon the country of Virginia because the little quarter wherein we are set down (unadvisedly so chosen) appears to be unwholesome and subject to many ill airs which accompany the like marish places.

[113]This passage is almost identical with one in the *True Declaration,* which is quoted, with omissions, at the end of Strachey's narrative. However, in the *Declaration* the number of settlers at the Falls is 100 rather than 400.

IV

The Lord La Warr's beginnings and proceedings in Jamestown; Sir Thomas Gates sent into England; his and the Company's testimony of Virginia and cause of the late miseries

---

PON His Lordship's landing at the south gate of the palisade (which looks into the river), our governor caused his company in arms to stand in order and make a guard. It pleased him that I should bear his colors for that time. His Lordship, landing, fell upon his knees and before us all made a long and silent prayer to himself, and after marched up into the town, where at the gate I bowed with the colors and let them fall at His Lordship's feet, who passed on into the chapel, where he heard a sermon by Master Bucke, our governor's preacher, and after that caused a gentleman, one of his own followers, Master Anthony Scot, his ancient, to read his commission, which entitled him lord governor and captain general during his life of the colony and plantation in Virginia (Sir Thomas Gates, our governor hitherto, being now styled therein lieutenant general).

After the reading of His Lordship's commission, Sir Thomas Gates rendered up unto His Lordship his own commission, both patents, and the council seal. After which the lord governor and captain general delivered some few words unto the company, laying many blames upon them for many vanities and their idleness, earnestly wishing that he might no more find it so lest he should be compelled to draw the sword of justice to cut off such delinquents, which he had much rather, he protested, draw in their defense to protect them from injuries; heartening them with the knowledge of what store of provisions he had brought for them, *viz.*, sufficient to serve four hundred men for one whole year.

The twelfth of June, being Tuesday, the lord governor and captain general did constitute and give places of office and charge to divers captains and gentlemen and elected unto him a council, unto whom he did administer an oath (mixed with the Oath of Allegiance and Supremacy to His Majesty; which oath likewise he caused to be administered the next day after to every particular member of the colony) of faith, assistance, and secrecy. The council which he elected were: Sir Thomas Gates, Knight, lieutenant general; Sir George Somers, Knight, admiral; Captain Percy, Esquire, and in the fort captain of fifty; Sir Ferdinando Wainman, Knight, master of the ordnance; Captain Christopher Newport, vice-admiral; William Strachey, Esquire, secretary and recorder.

As likewise the lord governor and captain general nominated Captain John Martin master of the battery works for steel and iron, and Captain George Webb sergeant major of the fort; and especial captains over companies were these appointed: Captain Edward Bruster, who hath the command of His Honor's own company, Captain Thomas Lawson, Captain Thomas Holecroft, Captain Samuel Argall, Captain George Yeardley, who commandeth the lieutenant general's company. Divers other officers were likewise made, as Master Ralph Hamor and Master Browne, clerks of the council, and Master Daniel Tucker and Master Robert Wilde, clerks of the store, etc.

The first business which the lord governor and captain general (after the settling of these officers) thought upon was to advise with his council for the obtaining of such provisions of victuals for store and quality as the country afforded. It did not appear that any kind of flesh, deer, or what else of that kind could be recovered from the Indian or to be sought in the country by the travail or search of his people and the old dwellers in the fort (together with the Indians not to friend[114]), who had the last winter destroyed and killed up all the hogs, insomuch as of five or six hundred (as it is supposed) there was not one left alive; nor an hen nor chick in the fort; and our horses and mares they had eaten with the first; and the provision which

[114]Unfriendly.

the lord governor and captain general had brought concerning any kind of flesh was little or nothing, in respect[115] it was not dreamt of by the adventurers in England that the swine were destroyed.

In council, therefore, the thirteenth of June, it pleased Sir George Somers, Knight, admiral, to propose a voyage, which, for the better relief and good of the colony, he would perform into the Bermudas, from whence he would fetch six months' provision of flesh and fish and some live hogs to store our colony again; and [he] had a commission given unto him the fifteenth of June, 1610, who in his own Bermuda pinnace, the "Patience," consorted with Captain Samuel Argall in the "Discovery" (whom the lord governor and captain general made of the council before his departure), the nineteenth of June fell with the tide from before our town and the twenty-second left the Bay or Cape Henry astern.

And likewise, because at the lord governor and captain general's first coming there was found in our own river no store of fish, after many trials the lord governor and captain general dispatched in the "Virginia" with instructions the seventeenth of June, 1610, Robert Tyndall, master of the "De La Warr," to fish unto, all along, and between Cape Henry and Cape Charles within the Bay; who the last of the said month returned unto us but as ill-speeding as the former, who our gov-

[115]Because.

ernor (now lieutenant general) had addressed thither before for the same purpose. Nor was the lord governor and captain general in the meanwhile idle at the fort, but every day and night he caused the nets to be hauled, sometimes a dozen times one after another. But it pleased not God so to bless our labors that we did at any time take one quarter so much as would give unto our people one pound at a meal apiece, by which we might have better husbanded our peas and oatmeal, notwithstanding the great store we now saw daily in our river. But let the blame of this lie where it is, both upon our nets and the unskillfulness of our men to lay them.

The sixth of July, Sir Thomas Gates, lieutenant general, coming down to Point Comfort, the north wind (blowing rough) he found had forced the longboat belonging to Algernon Fort to the other shore upon Nansemond side, somewhat short of Warrascoyack; which to recover again one of the lieutenant general's men, Humphrey Blunt, in an old canoe, made over; but the wind driving him upon the strand, certain Indians (watching the occasion) seized the poor fellow and led him up into the woods and sacrificed him. It did not a little trouble the lieutenant governor, who since his first landing in the country (how justly soever provoked) would not by any means be wrought to a violent proceeding against them for all the practices of villainy with which they daily endangered our men, thinking it possible by a more tractable course to win them to a better condition.[116] But now, being startled by this, he well perceived how little a fair and noble entreaty works upon a barbarous disposition and therefore in some measure purposed to be revenged.

The ninth of July he prepared his forces and early in the morning set upon a town of theirs, some four miles from Algernon Fort, called Kecoughtan, and had soon taken it, without loss or hurt of any of his men. The governor[117] and his women fled (the young King Powhatan's son not being there), but left his poor baggage and treasure to the spoil of our soldiers; which was only a few baskets of old wheat and some other of peas and beans, a little tobacco, and some few women's girdles of silk, of the grass silk, not without art and much neatness finely wrought; of which I have sent divers into England (being at the taking of the town), and would have sent Your Ladyship some of them, had they been a present so worthy.

We purposed to set a Frenchman here a-work to plant some vines, which grew naturally in great plenty.

[116]Purchas has a marginal rumination here: "Ad Graecas Calendas [i.e., never]. Can a leopard change his spots? Can a savage, remaining a savage, be civil? Were not we ourselves made and not born civil in our progenitors' days? And were not Caesar's Britons as brutish as Virginians? The Roman swords were best teachers of civility to this and other countries near us." Purchas reveals himself as one of the militant parsons who approved of forcible conversion.

[117]Indian commander of the town.

Some few cornfields it hath, and the corn in good forwardness, and we despair not but to be able (if our men
stand in health) to make it good against the Indian.

The continual practices of the subtle King Powhatan
doth not meanly[118] awaken all the powers and workings
of virtue and knowledge in our lord governor and captain general how to prevent not only his mischiefs but
to draw him upon some better terms and acknowledg-
ment of our forces and spirits, both able and daring to
quit him in any valiant and martial course whatsoever
he shall dare to run with us, which he doth yet scarcely
believe. For this therefore, since first, and that so
lately, he hath set on his people to attempt us with
private conspiracies and actual violence—into the one
drawing his neighbor confederates and underprinces,
and by the other working the loss and death of divers
of our men; and by such their loss, seizing their arms,
swords, pieces, etc., of which he hath gathered into his
store a great quantity and number, by intelligence above
two hundred swords, besides axes and poleaxes, chisels,
hoes to pare[119] and cleanse their ground, with an infinite
treasure of copper—our lord governor and captain
general sent two gentlemen with an embassy unto him,
letting him to understand of his practices and outrage
hitherto used toward our people, not only abroad but
at our fort also; yet flattering him withal how the lord

118Not meanly: to no small degree.
119Prepare.

governor and captain general did not suppose that these mischiefs were contrived by him or with his knowledge but conceived them rather to be the acts of his worst and unruly people. His Lordship, therefor now complaining unto him, required that he (being so great and wise a king) would give an universal order to his subjects that it might be no more so, lest the lord governor and captain general should be compelled (by defending him and his) to offend[120] him, which he would be loath to do. Withal he willed the messengers to demand of him, the said Powhatan, that he would either punish or send unto His Lordship such of his people whom Powhatan knew well not long before had assaulted our men at the blockhouse and but newly killed four of them, as also to demand of Powhatan, willing him to return unto the English fort both such men as he detained of ours and such arms as he had of theirs in his possession; and those conditions performed, he willed them to assure unto Powhatan that then their great werowance, the lord governor and captain general, would hold fair quarter and enter friendship with him, as a friend to King James and his subjects. But, refusing to submit to these demands, the lord governor and captain general gave in charge to the messengers so sent to signify unto Powhatan that His Lordship would by all means public and private seek to recover from him such of the English as he had, being subjects to his king and master,

[120]Injure.

unto whom even Powhatan himself had formerly vowed
not only friendship but homage, receiving from His
Majesty therefor many gifts and upon his knees a
crown and scepter, with other ornaments, the symbols
of civil state and Christian sovereignty, thereby obliging
himself to offices of duty to His Majesty.[121]

Unto all which Powhatan returned no other answer
but that either we should depart his country or confine
ourselves to Jamestown only, without searching further
up into his land or rivers, or otherwise he would give in
command to his people to kill us and do unto us all the
mischief which they at their pleasure could and we
feared; withal forewarning the said messengers not to
return any more unto him, unless they brought him a
coach and three horses, for he had understood by the
Indians which were in England how such was the state
of great werowances and lords in England, to ride and
visit other great men.

After this, divers times and daily he sent sometimes
two, sometimes three, unto our fort, to understand our

[121]The coronation, which took place in 1608, is described by Captain
John Smith in *A Map of Virginia . . . Whereunto Is Annexed the Proceedings of Those Colonies* (1612). Powhatan was presented with a
basin, ewer, bed, and furnishings, a scarlet cloak, and a crown. There
was some difficulty in persuading him to kneel to be crowned, but at
length, "by leaning hard on his shoulders, he a little stooped, and
Newport put the crown on his head." Feeling that some reciprocation
was in order, the king gave his old shoes and mantle to Captain Newport. See Edward Arber, *The Travels and Works of Captain John
Smith* (Edinburgh, 1910), I, 121-25, for a modern reprint.

strength and to observe our watch and guard, and how
our people stood in health, and what numbers were
arrived with this new werowance. Which being soon
perceived, our lord governor and captain general fore-
warned such his spies, upon their own peril, to resort
no more unto our fort. Howbeit, they would daily
press into our blockhouse and come up to our palisade
gates, supposing the government as well now as fantas-
tical and negligent [as] in the former times; the whilst,
some quarter of a mile short of the blockhouse, the
greatest number of them would make assault and lie in
ambush about our glasshouse, whither divers times,
indeed, our men would make out either to gather straw-
berries or to fetch fresh water: any one of which so
straggled, if they could with conveniency, they would
assault and charge with their bows and arrows, in which
manner they killed many of our men. Two of which,
being Paspaheans, who were ever our deadliest enemies
and not to be reconciled, at length being apprehended
(and one of them a notable villain, who had attempted
upon many in our fort), the lord governor caused them
to be manacled and convented before him and his council, where it was determined that he that had done so
much mischief should have his right hand struck off,
sending him away withal with a message to Powhatan
that unless he would yet return such Englishmen as he
detained, together with all such their arms (as before
spoken of), that not only the other (now prisoner)

should die, but all such of his savages as the lord governor and captain general could by any means surprise should run the same course; as likewise the lord governor and captain general would fire all his neighbor cornfields, towns, and villages, and that suddenly, if Powhatan sent not to contract with him the sooner.

What this will work with him, we know not as yet, for this was but the day before our ships were now falling to Point Comfort and so to set sail for England. Which ships, riding before Warrascoyack to take in their freight of cedar, clapboard, black walnut, and iron ore, took prisoners likewise the chief king of Warrascoyack, called Sasenticum, with his son Kainta and one of his chief men. And the fifteenth day of July, in the "Blessing," Captain Adams brought them to Point Comfort, where at that time (as well to take his leave of the lieutenant general, Sir Thomas Gates, now bound for England, as to dispatch the ships) the lord governor and captain general had pitched his tent in Algernon Fort.

The king's son, Kainta, the lord governor and captain general hath sent now into England until the ships arrive here again the next spring, dismissing the old werowance and the other with all terms of kindness and friendship, promising further designs to be effected by him, to which he hath bound himself by divers savage ceremonies and admirations.

And thus (right noble Lady) once more this famous

business, as recreated and dipped anew into life and spirit, hath raised it (I hope) from infamy and shall redeem the stains and losses under which she hath suffered since her first conception. Your graces still accompany the least appearance of her and vouchsafe her to be limned out with the beauty which we will beg and borrow from the fair lips. Nor fear you that she will return blushes to your cheeks for praising her, since (more than most excellent Lady) like yourself (were all tongues dumb and envious) she will praise herself in her most silence, may she once be but seen or but her shadow lively by a skillful workman set out indeed, which here (bungerly[122] as I am) I have presumed (though defacing it) in these papers to present unto Your Ladyship.

After Sir Thomas Gates his arrival, a book called *A True Declaration of Virginia* was published by the Company, out of which I have here inserted this their public testimony of the causes of the former evils and Sir Thomas Gates his report upon oath of Virginia.[123]

The ground of all those miseries was the permissive Providence of God, Who in the forementioned violent storm separated the head from the body, all the vital powers of regiment

---

[122]Bungling.

[123]The rest of the narrative is a verbatim quotation from *A True Declaration of the Estate of the Colony in Virginia* (London, 1610), with omissions here and there, as indicated by ellipsis dots. This was reprinted in *Tracts and Other Papers,* edited by Peter Force, III (Washington, D. C., 1844; New York, 1947), 3-27. Since the *Declara-*

being exiled with Sir Thomas Gates in those infortunate (yet fortunate) islands. The broken remainder of those supplies made a greater shipwreck in the continent of Virginia by the tempest of dissension: every man, overvaluing his own worth, would be a commander; every man, underprizing another's value, denied to be commanded. . . .[124]

The next fountain of woes was secure[125] negligence and improvidence, when every man sharked for his present booty but was altogether careless of succeeding penury. Now, I demand whether Sicilia or Sardinia (sometimes the barns of Rome) could hope for increase without manuring? A colony is therefore denominated because they should be *coloni,* the tillers of the earth and stewards of fertility. Our mutinous loiterers would not sow with providence, and therefore they reaped the fruits of too-dear-bought repentance. An incredible example of their idleness is the report of Sir Thomas Gates, who affirmeth that after his first coming thither he hath seen some of them eat their fish raw rather than they would go a stone's cast to fetch wood and dress it. *Dei laboribus omnia vendunt:* God sells us all things for our labor; when Adam himself might not live in Paradise without dressing the garden.

Unto idleness you may join treasons, wrought by those unhallowed creatures that forsook the colony and exposed their desolate brethren to extreme misery. You shall know that eight-

tion was not entered in the Stationers' Register until November 8, 1610, Strachey could not have had a printed copy at the time he wrote his letter to the "noble lady" in July, so presumably Samuel Purchas tacked this long quotation onto Strachey's narrative.

[124]Here the *Declaration* contains an irrelevant passage, citing classical analogies of insubordination, which is omitted by Purchas.

[125]Overconfident.

and-twenty or thirty of the company were appointed (in the ship called the "Swallow") to truck for corn with the Indians, and, having obtained a great quantity by trading, the most seditious of them, conspired together, persuaded some and enforced others to this barbarous project. They stole away the ship, they made a league amongst themselves to be professed pirates, with dreams of mountains of gold and happy robberies. Thus at one instant they wronged the hopes and subverted the cares of the colony, who, depending upon their return, forslowed[126] to look out for further provision. They created the Indians our implacable enemies by some violence they had offered; they carried away the best ship (which should have been a refuge in extremities); they weakened our forces by subtraction of their arms and succors.

These are that scum of men that, sailing in their piracy, that, being pinched with famine and penury, after their wild roving upon the sea, when all their lawless hopes failed, some remained with other pirates they met upon the sea, the others resolved to return for England, bound themselves by mutual oath to agree all in one report to discredit the land, to deplore the famine, and to protest that this their coming away proceeded from desperate necessity. These are they that roared out the tragical history of the man eating of his dead wife in Virginia, when the master of this ship willingly confessed before forty witnesses that at their coming away they left three months' victuals and all the cattle living in the Fort. Sometimes they reported that they saw this horrible action, sometimes that Captain Davies said so, sometimes that one Beadle, the lieutenant of Captain Davies, did relate it, varying this report into diversity of false

[126]Neglected.

colors which hold no likeness and proportion. But to clear all doubts, Sir Thomas Gates thus relateth the tragedy.

"There was one of the company who mortally hated his wife and therefore secretly killed her, then cut her in pieces and hid her in divers parts of his house. When the woman was missing, the man [was] suspected, his house searched, and parts of her mangled body were discovered. To excuse himself he said that his wife died, that he hid her to satisfy his hunger, and that he fed daily upon her. Upon this, his house was again searched, where they found a good quantity of meal, oatmeal, beans, and peas. He thereupon was arraigned, confessed the murder, and was burned for his horrible villainy."

Now shall the scandalous reports of a viperous generation preponderate the testimonies of so worthy leaders? Shall their venomous tongues blast the reputation of an ancient and worthy peer, who upon the ocular certainty of future blessings hath protested in his letters that he will sacrifice himself for his country in this service, if he may be seconded; and if the company do give it over, he will yet lay all his fortunes upon the prosecution of the plantation? . . .

Unto treasons you may join covetousness in the mariners; who for their private lucre partly embezzled the provisions, partly prevented our trade with the Indians, making the matches in the night and forestalling our market in the day, whereby the Virginians were glutted with our trifles and enhanced the prices of their corn and victual. That copper which before would have provided a bushel would not now obtain so much as a pottle. . . .

Join unto these another evil: there is great store of fish in the river, especially of sturgeon, but our men provided no more of them than for present necessity, not barreling up any store against that season the sturgeon returned to the sea. And not to dissemble their folly, they suffered fourteen nets (which was all they had) to rot and spoil, which by orderly drying and mending might have been preserved, but, being lost, all help of fishing perished. . . .

The state of the colony by these accidents began to find a sensible[127] declining; which Powhatan (as a greedy vulture) observing, and boiling with desire of revenge, he invited Captain Ratcliff and about thirty others to trade for corn, and under the color of fairest friendship he brought them within the compass of his ambush, whereby they were cruelly murdered and massacred. For, upon confidence of his fidelity, they went one and one into several houses, which caused their several destructions, when if but any six had remained together they would have been a bulwark for the general preservation. After this, Powhatan in the night cut off some of our boats; he drave away all the deer into the farther part of the country; he and his people destroyed our hogs (to the number of about six hundred); he sent none of his Indians to trade with us but laid secret ambushes in the woods, that if one or two dropped out of the fort alone they were endangered.

Cast up the reckoning together: want of government, store of idleness, their expectations frustrated by the traitors, their market spoiled by the mariners, our nets broken, the deer chased, our boats lost, our hogs killed, our trade with the Indians forbidden, some of our men fled, some murdered, and most by drinking of the brackish water of James Fort weakened and endangered, famine and sickness by all these means in-

[127]Appreciable.

creased; here at home the moneys came in so slowly that the
Lord La Warr could not be dispatched till the colony was
worn and spent with difficulties; above all, having neither ruler
nor preacher, they neither feared God nor man, which provoked
the wrath of the Lord of Hosts and pulled down His judgments upon them. *Discite justitiam moniti. . . .*

The Council of Virginia (finding the smallness of that return, which they hoped would have defrayed the charge of a
new supply) entered into a deep consultation and propounded
amongst themselves whether it were fit to enter into a new
contribution[128] or in time to send for home the Lord La Warr
and to abandon the action. They resolved to send for Sir
Thomas Gates, who being come, they adjured him to deal
plainly with them and to make a true relation of those things
which were presently to be had or hereafter to be hoped for
in Virginia. Sir Thomas Gates with a solemn and sacred oath
replied that all things before reported were true: that the
country yielded abundance of wood, as oak, wainscot, walnut
trees, bay trees, ash, sassafras, live oak, green all the year, cedar,
and fir: which are the materials of soap ashes and potashes, of
oils of walnuts, and bays, of pitch and tar, of clapboards, pipe
staves, masts and excellent boards of forty, fifty, and sixty
length and three-foot breadth, when one fir tree is able to make
the main mast of the greatest ship in England. He avouched
that there are incredible variety of sweet woods, especially of
the balsamum tree, which distilleth a precious gum; that there
are innumerable white mulberry trees, which in so warm a
climate may cherish and feed millions of silkworms and return

[128]Enter into a new contribution: i.e., subscribe additional funds for
the plantation.

us in a very short time as great a plenty of silk as is vented into the whole world from all the parts of Italy; that there are divers sorts of minerals, especially of iron ore lying upon the ground for ten miles' circuit (of which we have made a trial at home, that it maketh as good iron as any is in Europe) ; that a kind of hemp or flax and silk grass do grow there naturally, which will afford stuff for all manner of excellent cordage; that the river swarmeth with all manner of sturgeon; the land aboundeth with vines; the woods do harbor exceeding store of beavers, foxes, and squirrels; the waters do nourish a great increase of otters, all which are covered with precious furs; that there are in present discovered dyes and drugs of sundry qualities; that the oranges which have been planted did prosper in the winter, which is an infallible argument that lemons, sugar canes, almonds, rice, aniseed, and all other commodities which we have from the Straits, may be supplied to us in our own country and by our own industry; that the corn yieldeth a treble increase more than ours; and lastly, that it is one of the goodliest countries under the sun, interveined with five main rivers and promising as rich entrails as any kingdom of the earth to whom the sun is no nearer a neighbor.

*A Discovery of the Bermudas, Otherwise Called
the Isle of Devils*
(1610)

By Silvester Jourdain

A DISCOVERY...

BEING in [a] ship called the "Sea Venture," with Sir Thomas Gates our governor, Sir George Somers, and Captain Newport, three most worthy, honored gentlemen (whose valor and fortitude the world must needs take notice of, and that in most honorable designs) bound for Virginia, in the height of 30 degrees of northerly latitude or thereabouts we were taken with a most sharp and cruel storm upon the five-and-twentieth day of July, anno 1609, which did not only separate us from the residue of our fleet (which were eight in number), but with the violent working of the seas our ship became so shaken, torn, and leaked that she received so much water as covered two tier of hogsheads above the ballast; that our men stood up to the middles with buckets, barricos, and kettles to bail out the water and continually pumped for three days and three nights together without any intermission; and yet the water seemed rather to increase than to diminish. Insomuch that all our men, being utterly spent, tired, and disabled for longer labor, were even re- solved, without any hope of their lives, to shut up the hatches and to have committed themselves to the mercy of the sea (which is said to be merciless), or rather to the mercy of their mighty God and redeemer (whose mercies exceed all His works), seeing no help nor hope in the apprehension of man's reason that any mother's child would escape that inevitable danger, which every man had proposed and digested to himself, of present sinking. So that some of them, having some good and comfortable waters in the ship, fetched them and drunk one to the other, taking their last leave one of the other until their more joyful and happy meeting in a more blessed world; when it pleased God out of His most gracious and merciful providence so to direct and guide our ship (being left to the mercy of the sea) for her most advantage that Sir George Somers (sitting upon the poop of the ship, where he sate three days and three nights together, without meal's meat and [with] little or no sleep), conning[1] the ship to keep her as upright as he could (for otherwise she must needs instantly have foundered), most wishedly-happily descried land. Whereupon he most comfortably encouraged the com- pany to follow their pumping and by no means to cease bailing out of the water with their buckets, barricos, and kettles; whereby they were so overwearied, and their spirits so spent with long fasting and continuance of

[1]I.e., keeping a lookout and directing the steersman.

their labor, that for the most part they were fallen
asleep in corners and wheresoever they chanced first to
sit or lie; but, hearing news of land, wherewith they
grew to be somewhat revived, being carried with will
and desire beyond their strength, every man bustled up
and gathered his strength and feeble spirits together to
perform as much as their weak force would permit him;
through which weak means it pleased God to work so
strongly as the water was stayed for that little time
(which, as we all much feared, was the last period of
our breathing) and the ship kept from present sinking,
when it pleased God to send her within half an English
mile of that land that Sir George Somers had not long
before descried, which were the islands of the Bermudas.

And there neither did our ship sink but, more fortu-
nately in so great a misfortune, fell in between two
rocks, where she was fast lodged and locked for further
budging; whereby we gained not only sufficient time,
with the present help of our boat and skiff, safely to set
and convey our men ashore (which were 150 in number) but afterwards had time and leisure to save some
good part of our goods and provision, which the water
had not spoiled, with all the tacking of the ship and
much of the iron about her, which were necessaries not
a little available[2] for the building and furnishing of a
new ship and pinnace, which we made there for the
transporting and carrying of us to Virginia. But our
delivery was not more strange, in falling so opportunely

[2]Advantageous.

and happily upon the land, as our feeding and preservation was beyond our hopes and all men's expectations most admirable.[3]

For the islands of the Bermudas, as every man knoweth that hath heard or read of them, were never inhabited by any Christian or heathen people but ever esteemed and reputed a most prodigious and enchanted place, affording nothing but gusts, storms, and foul weather, which made every navigator and mariner to avoid them as Scylla and Charybdis, or as they would shun the Devil himself; and no man was ever heard to make for the place but as, against their wills, they have by storms and dangerousness of the rocks, lying seven leagues unto the sea, suffered shipwreck. Yet did we find there the air so temperate and the country so abundantly fruitful of all fit necessaries for the sustentation and preservation of man's life that, most in a manner of all our provisions of bread, beer, and victual being quite spoiled in lying long drowned in salt water, notwithstanding we were there for the space of nine months (few days over or under) not only well received, comforted, and with good satiety contented, but out of the abundance thereof provided us some reasonable quantity and proportion of provision to carry us for Virginia and to maintain ourselves and that company we found there, to the great relief of them, as it fell out, in their so great extremities and, in respect of the shortness of time, until it pleased God that by My

[3]Wonderful.

Lord's coming thither their store was better supplied. And greater and better provisions we might have made if we had had better means for the storing and transportation thereof. Wherefore my opinion sincerely of this island is that whereas it hath been and is still accounted the most dangerous, infortunate, and most forlorn place of the world, it is in truth the richest, healthfullest, and pleasing land (the quantity and bigness thereof considered) and merely natural, as ever man set foot upon. The particular profits and benefits whereof shall be more especially inserted and hereunto annexed, which every man to his own private knowledge, that was there, can avouch and justify for a truth.

Upon the eight-and-twentieth day of July, 1609 (after the extremity of the storm was something qualified), we fell upon the shore at the Bermudas; where after our general, Sir Thomas Gates, Sir George Somers, and Captain Newport had by their provident carefulness landed all their men and so much of the goods and provisions out of the ship as was not utterly spoiled, every man disposed and applied himself to search for and to seek out such relief and sustentation as the country afforded. And Sir George Somers, a man inured to extremities (and knowing what thereunto belonged) was in this service neither idle nor backward but presently by his careful industry went and found out sufficient of many kind of fishes, and so plentiful thereof that in half an hour he took so many great fishes with hooks as did suffice the whole company one day. And

fish is there so abundant that if a man step into the
water they will come round about him; so that men
were fain to get out for fear of biting. These fishes are
very fat and sweet and of that proportion and bigness
that three of them will conveniently lade two men:
those we called rockfish. Besides there are such abundance of mullets that with a seine might be taken at one
draught one thousand at the least; and infinite store of
pilchards; with divers kinds of great fishes, the names
of them unknown to me; of crayfishes very great ones
and so great store as that there hath been taken in one
night with making lights even sufficient to feed the
whole company a day. The country affordeth great
abundance of hogs, as that there hath been taken by
Sir George Somers, who was the first hunted for them,
to the number of two-and-thirty at one time, which he
brought to the company in a boat built by his own
hands.

There is fowl in great num[ber] upon the islands
where they breed, that there hath been taken in two or
three hours a thousand at the least, the bird being of
the bigness of a good pigeon and layeth eggs as big as
hen eggs upon the sand, where they come and lay them
daily although men sit down amongst them, that there
hath been taken up in one morning by Sir Thomas
Gates's men one thousand of eggs; and Sir George
Somers' men, coming a little distance of time after
them, have stayed there whilst they came and laid their
eggs amongst them, that they brought away as many

more with them, with many young birds very fat and sweet.

Another seafowl there is that lieth in little holes in the ground, like unto a cony hole, and are in great numbers, exceeding good meat, very fat and sweet (those we had in the winter) and their eggs are white and of that bigness that they are not to be known from hen eggs. The other bird's eggs are speckled and of a different color. There are also great store and plenty of herons, and those so familiar and tame that we beat them down from the trees with stones and staves—but such were young herons—besides many white herons without so much as a black or grey feather on them; with other small birds so tame and gentle that, a man walking in the woods with a stick and whistling to them, they will come and gaze on you, so near that you may strike and kill many of them with your stick; and with singing and holloing you may do the like.

There are also great store of tortoises (which some call turtles) and those so great that I have seen a bushel of eggs in one of their bellies, which are sweeter than any hen egg; and the tortoise itself is all very good meat and yieldeth great store of oil, which is as sweet as any butter; and one of them will suffice fifty men a meal, at the least; and of these hath been taken great store, with two boats, at the least forty in one day.

The country yieldeth divers fruits, as prickled pears, great abundance, which continue green upon the trees all the year; also great plenty of mulberries, white and red, and on the same are great store of silkworms, which yield cods of silk, both white and yellow, being some coarse and some fine.

And there is a tree called a palmetto tree, which hath a very sweet berry upon which the hogs do most feed; but our men, finding the sweetness of them, did willingly share with the hogs for them, they being very pleasant and wholesome, which made them careless almost of any bread with their meat; which occasioned us to carry in a manner all that store of flour and meal we did or could save for Virginia. The head of the palmetto tree is very good meat, either raw or sodden; it yieldeth a head which weigheth about twenty pound and is far better meat than any cabbage.

There are an infinite number of cedar trees (the fairest, I think, in the world) and those bring forth a very sweet berry and wholesome to eat.

The country (forasmuch as I could find myself or hear by others) affords no venomous creature, or so much as a rat or mouse or any other thing unwholesome.

There is great store of pearl, and some of them very fair, round, and oriental,[4] and you shall find at least one hundred seed of pearl in one oyster. There hath been likewise found some good quantity of ambergris, and that of the best sort. There are also great plenty of whales, which I conceive are very easy to be killed, for

[4]Lustrous.

they come so usually and ordinarily to the shore that we heard them oftentimes in the night abed and have seen many of them near the shore in the daytime.

There was born upon the Bermudas, at the time of our being there, two children, the one a man-child, there baptized by the name of Bermudas, and a woman-child, baptized by the name of Bermuda; as also there was a marriage between two English people upon the island. This island, I mean the main island, with all the broken islands adjacent, are made in the form of a half moon, but a little more rounder, and divided into many broken islands, and there are many good harbors in it; but we could find [only] one especial place to go in, or rather to go out from it, which was not altogether free from some danger, and that lieth on the southeast side, where there is three fathoms water at the entrance thereof, but within six, seven, or eight fathoms at the least, where you may safely be landlocked from the danger of all winds and weathers, and more to the trees. The coming into it is so narrow and strait between the rocks as that it will with small store of munition be fortified and easily defended with all advantage the place affords against the forces of the potentest king of Europe.

There are also plenty of hawks and very good tobacco, as I think, which through forgetfulness I had almost omitted.

Now, having finished and rigged our ship and pinnace, the one called the "Deliverance," the pinnace the "Patience," we prepared and made ourselves ready to ship for Virginia, having powdered[5] some store of hogs' flesh for provision thither and the company thereof for some reasonable time but were compelled to make salt there for the same purpose, for all our salt was spent and spoiled before we recovered the shore. We carried with us also a good portion of tortoise oil, which either for frying or baking did us very great pleasure, it being very sweet, nourishing, and wholesome.

The greatest defects we found there was tar and pitch for our ship and pinnace, instead whereof we were forced to make lime there of a hard kind of stone and use it, which for the present occasion and necessity, with some wax we found cast up by the sea from some shipwreck, served the turn to pay[6] the seams of the pinnace Sir George Somers built, for which he had neither pitch nor tar.

So that God, in the supplying of all our wants beyond all measure, showed Himself still merciful unto us, that we might accomplish our intended voyage to Virginia, for which I confidently hope He doth yet reserve a blessing in store, and to the which I presume every honest and religious heart will readily give their Amen.

When all things were made ready and commodiously fitted, the wind coming fair, we set sail and put off from

[5]Salted.
[6]Cover with tar or the like.

the Bermudas the tenth of May in the year 1610, and arrived at Jamestown in Virginia the four-and-twentieth day of the same month, where we found some three-score persons living. And being then some three weeks or thereabouts past, and not hearing of any supply, it was thought fitting by a general consent to use the best means for the preservation of all those people that were living, being all in number two hundred persons. And so, upon the eighth of June, 1610, we embarked at Jamestown, not having above fourteen days' victual, and so were determined to direct our course for New-foundland, there to refresh us and supply ourselves with victual to bring us home.

But it pleased God to dispose otherwise of us and to give us better means. For being all of us shipped in four pinnaces and departed from the town, almost down half the river, we met My Lord De La Warr coming by with three ships well furnished with victual, which revived all the company and gave them great content. And after some few days My Lord, under-standing of the great plenty of hogs and fish was at the Bermudas and the necessity of them in Virginia, was desirous to send thither to supply himself with those things for the better comforting of his men and the plantation of the country.

Whereupon Sir George Somers, being a man best acquainted with the place, and being willing to do ser-vice unto his prince and country without any respect of his own private gain, and being of threescore years of age at the least, out of his worthy and valiant mind offered himself to undertake to perform with God's help that dangerous voyage for the Bermudas, for the better relief and comfort of the people in Virginia and for the better plantation of it; which offer My Lord De La Warr very willingly and thankfully accepted. And so upon the nineteenth of June Sir George Somers embarked himself at Jamestown in a small barge of thirty ton or thereabout that he built at the Bermudas, wherein he labored from morning until night, as duly as any workman doth labor for wages, and built her all with cedar, with little or no ironwork at all, having in her but one bolt, which was in the kelson.[7] Notwithstanding, thanks be to God, she brought us in safety to Virginia, and so I trust He will protect him and send him well back again, to his heart's desire and the great comfort of all the company there.[8]

The Bermudas lieth in the height of 32½ degrees of northerly latitude, Virginia bearing directly from it, west-northwest, 230 leagues.

[7] A line of timbers bolted to the keel to secure it to the floor timbers.

[8] Somers reached Bermuda safely after battling a storm, only to die there shortly afterward "of a surfeit in eating a pig," according to Edmund Howes's continuation of the *Annals of John Stow* (1614), p. 942. See also the *Dictionary of National Biography*.

A VOYAGE TO VIRGINIA IN 1609
was printed by The Dietz Press, Inc.
for the University Press of Virginia
Types used were Intertype Caslon Oldstyle
and American Caslon
The paper is Permalife Text
manufactured by the Standard Paper Company
Binding is by Williams Printing Company
The book is designed by John J. Walklet, Jr.